NATIONAL
GEOGRAPHIC
KiDS

Beneath the Waves

CELEBRATING the OCEAN through PICTURES, POEMS, and STORIES

STEPHANIE WARREN DRIMMER

NATIONAL GEOGRAPHIC
WASHINGTON, D.C.

CONTENTS

Foreword

A day at the beach was absolutely magical when I was a young boy. It was a pretty long car ride to get to the ocean, and I couldn't wait to get out of there and run into the water. Living in New England, that water was always a little chilly, but I didn't care. I just needed to submerge myself in those waves. The longer I spent in the water or the more seaweed I touched brought me closer to this place that beckoned me to explore. The ocean was like an old friend that I hadn't seen for a while and needed to hug. I remember looking out at the expansive seascape and wondering what might be discovered beneath those waves. Staring at the sea stirred my soul and ignited within me a passion to explore. It seemed to be a place of endless discoveries and adventures, and I yearned to journey farther, out beyond the water's edge.

When I was in my teens, I became a scuba diver and then an underwater photographer. Since then I have spent my life exploring the sea with a camera, making pictures and sharing stories of all that I have learned. I have been nose-to-nose with sharks on tropical coral reefs and dived with seals beneath 25-foot (7.6-m)-thick ice. I have spent days photographing shrimps smaller than a grain of rice that were living on anemones and hours swimming with whales that allowed me into their world.

The experiences I have had with ocean wildlife have been beyond my wildest childhood dreams. I often think of my life as an endless string of extraordinary moments in nature. I have fallen in love with being in the company of ocean animals and seeing the amazing ways they live. After decades of undersea exploration, I realize that I have only scratched the surface of what remains to be seen. The majority of ocean realms and the species that exist there are waiting to be discovered. Given that every other breath we take comes from oxygen created by organisms in the ocean, it is vital that we explore and protect it.

As you read *Beneath the Waves,* you will find yourself on an undersea odyssey, with each chapter revealing a rich tapestry of life that is connected to all others. Your undersea exploration begins here!

—Brian Skerry

Brian Skerry is a photojournalist specializing in marine wildlife. Since 1998 he has been a contract photographer for *National Geographic* magazine covering a wide range of subjects and stories. In 2014 he was named a National Geographic Fellow. He has published more than 25 stories for *National Geographic* magazine on a range of subjects from sharks and whales to dolphins and coral reefs. Brian's work has also been featured in publications such as the *New York Times, BBC Wildlife, Paris Match,* the *Washington Post,* the *Wall Street Journal, Smithsonian, Esquire, Audubon,* and *Men's Journal.* Brian is the author of 10 books, including the acclaimed *Ocean Soul* and his latest monograph, entitled *SHARK.* You can follow his work on Instagram (@BrianSkerry).

OCEAN PLANET

When we think of Earth, many of us think of land. After all, land is where we build our homes and make friends and go to school. It's where we walk and run and live. We can see and explore so much of it—from tall mountains to deep valleys, from deserts to lush rainforests, from rocky canyons to vast plains. But Earth is so much more than just land.

The ocean is vast, and except for the slim surface layer, it is cold and dark. Humans can't easily explore the undersea world: To get even a glimpse, we need goggles and snorkels, wet suits and air tanks, deep-sea submersibles and underwater robots. And so, much of the ocean remains a mystery to us.

Yet Earth is undeniably a world of water. The ocean covers more than 70 percent of the planet's surface. We depend on it for our climate, much of our food, and even the oxygen we need to breathe. And though humans can't live under the sea, many of our planet's fellow creatures can: The ocean makes up an amazing 99 percent of all space on Earth where it's possible for life to exist.

Scientists believe that life on our planet originated in the oceans. So it's no surprise that the seas are home to most of Earth's plants and animals. The variety of living things that float, swim, and dive in the oceans is truly astounding. There are teeny plankton, most too small to see, that drift with the currents. There are enormous blue whales, the biggest creatures that have ever lived. There are rainbow-colored coral reef animals, schools of fish that swim together by the millions, turtles that migrate from one end of Earth to another, and deep-sea fish so strange they look like aliens.

From low tide on the beach to the open ocean, from icy polar regions to underwater meadows, from the sunlit surface to the endless, cold darkness near the seafloor, the ocean is teeming with beings unlike anything we can see on land. And it's just waiting to be explored.

So let's wade in. No gear required!

Beneath the Waves

The world that lies beneath the waves
Abounds unfathomably deep
With secrets that the reefs and caves
And ocean trenches strive to keep.

But most amazing is the cast
Of creatures who are living there,
So many still unknown. The vast
Abyss is one gigantic lair.

Sharks, jellyfish, blue whales, and all
The marvels of this waterpark,
Inhabitants both large and small
Patrol the desert of the dark.

Submersibles have shed some light
On life-forms in this biosphere:
They swim out of the gloom of night,
And just as quickly disappear.

And if you want to see much more,
Let your imagination spend
An hour on the ocean floor
Gazing at wonders without end.

—J. Patrick Lewis

9

IN THE ZONES

From the surface, the ocean may seem like nothing more than a vast pool of water. But sink beneath the waves and head downward, and you'll find that as you move deeper, the ocean changes. The temperature drops and the pressure increases, making each ocean depth its own unique environment. Scientists have divided the ocean into three main layers, called zones.

The Sunlit Zone

This shallow zone extends down to a maximum depth of about 650 feet (200 m). Here, the sun shines through the water, bringing light and warmth. There is enough light for plants to make energy from the sunlight, just like they do on land. These plants are a source of food for all kinds of animals, such as jellyfish, tuna, sharks, and dolphins.

The Twilight Zone

This zone extends from the sunlit zone down to about 3,300 feet (1,000 m). Here, the light of the sun is very dim. In these murky waters live creatures such as whales, cuttlefish, swordfish, and squid. Since there is much less food here than in the sunny waters above, some animals that live in this zone rise toward the surface to eat.

The Midnight Zone

This is the deepest zone of the ocean, extending from the edge of the twilight zone down to the seafloor. Here, there is no light at all. The waters are eternally pitch black and extremely cold. The weight of all that water above means the pressure is also extreme. Despite these harsh conditions, animals live here, too—strange ones such as see-through squid, glowing lanternfish, and monster-size giant squid.

On the Beach

Seagulls wheel high above, their gray wings fading into the sky. The air smells salty and wild. You step forward, feeling the warm sand sink beneath your toes. A wave skims across the shore, covering your feet in a rush of cool water. You're at the beach. Here is where the land—the world of humans—touches the world of the ocean. If you know where to look, you'll find that all kinds of creatures make their home here.

Sea Shell

Sea Shell, Sea Shell,
Sing me a song, O Please!
A song of ships, and sailor men,
And parrots, and tropical trees,
Of islands lost in the Spanish Main
Which no man ever may find again,
Of fishes and corals under the waves,
And seahorses stabled in great green caves.
Sea Shell, Sea Shell,
Sing of the things you know so well.

—Amy Lowell

ONE OF THE WORLD'S **OLDEST SHELL COLLECTIONS** WAS UNEARTHED FROM THE RUINS OF THE ANCIENT CITY OF POMPEII.

CONCH SHELL

Secrets of the Shell

They can be pink and curved like a baby's ear, sharp and spiny like a cactus, spotted and striped like animals of the African savanna. Seashells come in endless shapes, patterns, and colors. Humans are so fascinated by shells that some will spend hours searching the sand for the most beautiful specimens.

But before the wondrous seashell washed ashore, it had a past life—as body armor! Sea creatures such as snails, clams, and oysters grow shells to protect their soft and delicate bodies. Even after those animals' lives are over, their shells go on without them, becoming homes for the more than 800 species of hermit crab that shelter inside them.

The shape of a shell depends on where it comes from. Shells with spikes, bumps, and ridges usually come from tropical oceans. There, all kinds of plants and animals thrive in the warm water. That means that there are lots of fierce predators prowling for a meal. The more elaborate a creature's shell, the harder it is for a hungry hunter to crack into.

The colors and patterns of shells are no accident, either. Sometimes, a shell's appearance helps it survive. Mother-of-pearl—the shiny, iridescent coating on the inside of some shells—encases irritants or harmful invaders such as parasites, helping protect the creature that lives inside. The shell's colors and patterns can also act as camouflage—such as wavy lines that might help hide it among the leaves of a kelp forest. Still other times, a shell's design is for communication. Bright colors often act like warning labels, alerting predators that the creature inside is poisonous or icky-tasting. To a human, a shell's shiny surface or pastel hue might look beautiful—but to the animal who once lived there, it's a matter of life and death!

FEELING CRABBY

They wave their claws, twitch their antennae, and wiggle their stalk eyes. Crabs scurry and dig on beaches all over the world.

Coconut Crabs

Coconut crabs climb high into palm trees to reach their favorite food: coconuts. Their brown shells help conceal them against the palm trunks. The largest land crab on Earth, this crustacean can be three feet (0.9 m) across, and has claws strong enough to crack a coconut—or even break a bone.

Hermit Crabs

Hermit crabs are always growing—and that means they're always looking to upgrade to a larger shell. When a new one washes up onshore, a group of crabs will gather to see if it's a good fit. But only one can move in. So the crabs line up from biggest to smallest. When the largest crab steps out of its old shell, the next largest climbs in. This crab conga continues until everyone has a new house.

Halloween Crabs

Boo! It might look like this crab is dressed up in a colorful costume, but the orange-and-black shell is just the Halloween crab's everyday attire. This creature's lifestyle fits its creepy name: It's active in the dark of night, climbing trees and burrowing inside underground holes.

Atlantic Ghost Crabs

What's that burrowing on the beach? It's an Atlantic ghost crab, which shelters from the sun in underground hideaways up to four feet (1.2 m) deep. Its semi-transparent shell and pair of white claws might make the crab look like a specter in the sand, but they also help hide it from predators on the beach.

THESE CRABS LIVE ONLY ONE PLACE IN THE WORLD: CHRISTMAS ISLAND.

Red Crabs

Every spring, something incredible happens on Australia's Christmas Island: Millions of small, reddish crabs emerge from the forest and march together into the sea. Scuttling sideways, they cross open areas and shimmy down cliffs in never-ending red waves. To help the crabs make it to their ocean destination, the local people close down roads and have even built special crab tunnels.

WHAT IS THE BEACH?

You unfurl your beach towel and lay it down, ready for a fun day at the shore. But have you ever wondered how the beach you're running, digging, and playing on came to be?

The water that forms our oceans is ancient—older than Earth itself. Some of the ingredients of water came to be in the big bang, the moment around 13.8 billion years ago that created the universe and everything in it. The rest of the ingredients were made later, in stars. For billions of years after the universe was born, it was a huge cloud of swirling dust and rocks moving through space. Over time, some of this material came together to make planet Earth. And inside this rocky material were tiny droplets of water.

When Earth was young, about four billion years ago, it was very hot—so hot that the rocks melted and turned into glowing liquid. The water inside escaped as steam. The steam formed clouds, and the clouds rained down water. Some scientists think all of the water in Earth's oceans came to be this way. But others think some came from asteroids, rocky bodies often containing ice that zip through space. Many of them may have slammed into Earth and melted, adding water to the new oceans.

Sand was born from Earth's weather. Over millions of years, moving water and blowing wind wore away at our planet's rocks. Some rocks slowly broke down into smaller and smaller pieces. They rolled and tumbled down rivers and streams and, finally, to the ocean, where the waves and tides wore them down even more. From boulders to rocks to pebbles, they finally became sand. Today, the beach is a great place to visit on a summer vacation—but it also tells a story about the history of our planet!

"IN EVERY CURVING BEACH, IN EVERY GRAIN OF SAND, THERE IS A **STORY OF THE EARTH.**"
—Rachel Carson

WHETHER A
SEA TURTLE
IS MALE OR FEMALE IS
DETERMINED BY THE
TEMPERATURE OF ITS NESTING
ENVIRONMENT: COOLER
SAND PRODUCES MORE
MALES, AND WARMER SAND
PRODUCES MORE
FEMALES.

TINY TURTLES

When they're grown up, green sea turtles are mighty creatures. They paddle great distances with powerful flippers, are protected by enormous shells, and weigh as much as 440 pounds (200 kg).

But when sea turtles are first born, they're tiny and vulnerable. And it's then that they have to undertake the riskiest journey of their lives: waddling from the sand where they hatch to the safety of the waves.

A mother sea turtle digs a hole on the beach, lays her eggs inside, and covers them carefully. Then she goes back to her ocean home, leaving the eggs defenseless. After about two months, the turtles are ready to hatch. Using a temporary tooth called a caruncle, they chip their way through the shells. Then, using their tiny flippers, they slowly dig their way up out of the nest to the surface. That process is exhausting for a newborn. But the hardest part is yet to come: The little turtles have to make it down the beach to the sea, past waiting predators like birds, crabs, and raccoons.

Many baby turtles don't survive this journey. And only about one in 1,000 makes it all the way to adulthood. Besides predators, they face challenges from humans, including lights near the beach—from cars, campfires, and houses—that can confuse the hatchlings. Normally, they follow the light of the moon to navigate, but man-made lights can make them travel in the wrong direction. Despite these great odds, every year, on beaches all over the world, some turtles do survive. They scramble across the sand to the water, where they spend years growing to full size—and where most males will stay the rest of their lives. Finally, the day comes when the adult female sea turtles make the journey back to lay their own eggs on the beaches where they hatched.

HIDE-AND-SEEK

When the tide goes out, it leaves behind a smooth expanse of sand. The beach might look completely empty, but below the surface wiggle all kinds of creatures. These animals spend their lives moving up and down the beach, following the rising and falling tides.

Weevers

Some animals, like the weever, spend all day buried in the sand beneath shallow water with only their eyes showing. When small fish and shrimps swim by—snap!—the weever gets a meal. But when high tide comes in, the predator becomes prey to bigger fish that swim in from the sea.

Sand Mason Worms

For an animal without hands, a sand mason worm has impressive building abilities. Using bits of shell and sand, along with mucus to stick them together, the worm creates a tube-shaped structure to live inside. It uses its tangle of tentacles to snag plankton when the beach floods at high tide.

Sand Crabs

These critters are easy to spot at many beaches—just look for sand at the water's edge dotted with tiny holes. That's where sand crabs are hiding just under the surface, catching plankton in their antennae. As the waves wash away the sand, they have to constantly rebury themselves.

Razor Clams

Razor clams, Pismo clams, and others live in beach sand, coming to the surface at high tide to feed on plankton and other small, tasty bits. Most of the time, they keep their bodies hidden beneath the sand. The only sign they're there is a flexible food-gathering tube they poke above the surface, like a submarine's periscope.

Moon Snails

The largest living marine snail, the moon snail has a shell that can reach 5.5 inches (14 cm) across. Moon snails feed on another kind of shelled critter: clams. After firmly grasping a clam with its foot and dragging it into deep sand, the snail uses a toothed, tonguelike structure called a radula to bore a hole in the shell.

BEACH BIRDS

They run across the sand on long legs, chirping and chattering, on a constant hunt for tasty morsels to gobble up. Shorebirds feed on the marine creatures that make their homes beneath the sand on beaches across the globe.

MOST SHOREBIRDS
DON'T BUILD NESTS. THEY LAY THEIR EGGS ON A BIT OF FLAT SAND, ROCK, OR MEADOW.

Black-Necked Stilts

The extra-long legs of the black-necked stilt can make it look kind of silly when it's walking on land. But they're not only for show: The stilt's lengthy legs allow it to wade into deeper water than other birds to hunt.

Ruffs

At the beginning of the breeding season, male ruffs dress to impress, growing long feathers on their necks and heads. Then they perform an elaborate courtship dance, leaping into the air, bowing, crouching, and raising their head tufts for audiences of female ruffs. Nice moves!

Oystercatchers

These sneaky birds wait until the tide begins to carry the water out to sea. Then, the oysters, clams, and mussels they like to eat are holding their shells open to feed, making the meat inside easy for the birds to grab. If an oystercatcher fails to snag a snack that way, the bird simply uses its bright orange beak like a hammer to break open the shell.

Crab Plovers

These beachgoing birds lay their eggs right on the beach, in burrows they dig about five feet (1.5 m) deep in sandbanks. Crab plovers have extra-strong, heavy bills, which they use to crack open crab shells.

Roseate Spoonbills

Imagine having a spoon for a mouth. That's exactly what life is like for a spoonbill! These birds hold their bills slightly open and sweep them side to side below the surface of the water. This technique allows them to scoop up small animals like shrimps.

Why Is the Ocean Salty?

Since ancient times, people have observed something puzzling about Earth's waters: Our planet flows with freshwater lakes, rivers, and streams, which all lead to the sea. So why is the sea salty?

Long ago, people didn't have science to explain Earth's natural processes. So instead, they made up stories to make sense of the world around them. The people of the Philippines have a clever myth to explain the sea's saltiness. According to a traditional Filipino folktale, the ocean's water was once fresh. That changed when a fisherman visited a small island and came across an old machine. When he touched it, a genie came out! The genie explained that his machine could make salt—as much as the fisherman wanted. The fisherman could put it on his food and give it to his friends and family. The only thing he couldn't do was remove the machine from the island.

But, according to the folktale, the fisherman became greedy. Against the genie's wishes, he stole the machine, put it in his boat, and began to row home. The genie was furious. The genie turned on the machine and left it running. Salt filled the fisherman's buckets, then his boat, then spilled into the sea. And the machine didn't stop until the ocean was as salty as it is now.

Today, we know the true source of the ocean's salt: rocks. Because the rain that falls on land is slightly acidic, it gradually breaks down rocks, dissolving some of the minerals inside them. Rivers and streams carry these minerals to the ocean, where most of them are used up as nutrients by marine plants and animals. What's left behind is salt. Other salts have bubbled up into the sea from deep inside Earth. Over hundreds of millions of years, these processes caused the ocean's salt levels to rise until the sea became salty.

SALTY SEASHORE

SALT CRYSTALS
ON STONES

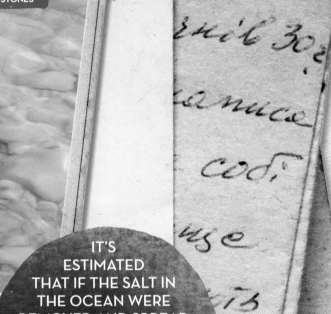

IT'S ESTIMATED THAT IF THE SALT IN THE OCEAN WERE REMOVED AND SPREAD EVENLY OVER EARTH'S LAND, IT WOULD FORM A LAYER THE HEIGHT OF **A 40-STORY** BUILDING.

A FISHERMAN IN THE PHILIPPINES

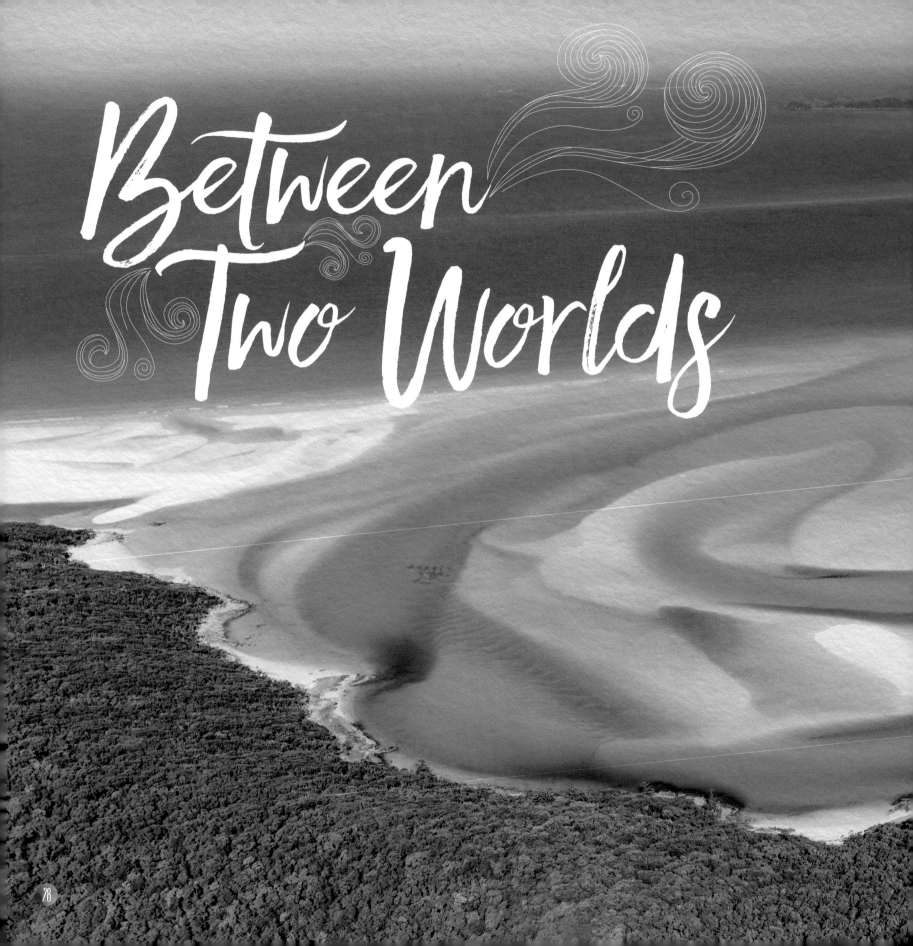

Between Two Worlds

You stand at the end of a river, where water that has traveled thousands of miles leaves the land and flows, at last, into the sea. Here, the water isn't quite fresh, and it isn't quite salty; it's a bit of both. Many animals make their home in this in-between place, from crawling crabs to wheeling birds to giant, ferocious saltwater crocodiles. They're not the only creatures that live between two worlds: Some of Earth's most astounding animals live between two worlds, clambering on land and diving beneath the waves.

ACHOO!
MARINE IGUANAS CAN OFTEN BE FOUND SPORTING **WHITE "WIGS."** THE IGUANAS SNEEZE THESE GLOBS OF SALT ONTO THEIR HEADS AND FACES.

THE SWIMMING LIZARD

"Their limbs and strong claws are admirably adapted for crawling over the rugged fissured masses of lava, which everywhere form the coast."

These were some of famed British naturalist Charles Darwin's observations of marine iguanas basking on the shores of the Galápagos Islands, after he arrived there in 1835 on the ship the H.M.S. *Beagle*. The amazing adaptations of these rare reptiles—with their stubby faces, knobby skin, and salt-crusted heads—helped him go on to unlock the mysteries of evolution that explain how Earth's animals change over time.

Marine iguanas are remarkable for being the only oceangoing lizards in the world. Scientists believe that the ancestors of these unique animals were land-dwelling iguanas from South America. They came to their current home by accident, when driftwood or other debris they were resting on washed out to sea. As it went, it took its accidental passengers hundreds of miles to the shores of the Galápagos, a chain of volcanic islands 600 miles (966 km) west of the mainland of Ecuador.

But the lizards' new home proved a harsh place to live: Other land iguanas on the Galápagos were stuck snacking mostly on cactus. So the newcomers looked for a new food source, and, luckily, there was lots of nutritious algae to eat. The only problem was, it grew underwater. So, over time, marine iguanas developed a whole host of tactics to help them get to their new meal.

Marine iguanas dive into the sea, using their webbed feet and flattened tails to propel themselves through the water. They cling to rocks with their long, sharp claws and use their small, sharp teeth to scrape off algae. The waters around the Galápagos are chilly—a serious challenge for a cold-blooded animal. So marine iguanas spend only a few hours a day feeding. The rest of the time they bask in the sun to warm up, their black skin helping them absorb as much warmth as they can.

HOW CAN YOU TELL SEALS AND SEA LIONS APART? A

TRUE SEAL

HAS ONLY HOLES ON THE SIDES OF ITS HEAD, WHILE A SEA LION HAS SMALL EARFLAPS.

SEALS SHARE THEIR ANCESTRY WITH **DOGS.**

Seals

Smooth by Sea

Although harbor seals breathe air, they spend about half their lives in the water. They are agile swimmers that use their flippers to speed through the sea and dive deep beneath the surface—sometimes spending 40 minutes below the waves!

Harbor seals can plunge to 1,500 feet (457 m) while on the hunt for their favorite foods, which include sole, flounder, cod, and octopus. During a deep dive, they can slow their heart rates to conserve oxygen, from 120 beats a minute to as few as three. Their blood is concentrated around their brain, heart, and lungs to keep these essential organs working while the seals swim far beneath the surface.

Harbor seals are skilled swimmers, but when it's time to return to shore, they're not nearly so graceful: Their flippers aren't adapted for moving on land, so the seals have to flop along on their bellies! Harbor seals can often be spotted resting on rocks, ice, sand, or mud with their head and rear flippers held up, giving their body a shape like a banana. During breeding season, huge numbers of harbor seals lumber their way onto land. Hundreds often gather along shores in the northern regions of the Atlantic and Pacific Oceans.

Seal pups are born ready for the water, and most can already swim and dive only a few hours after birth. Harbor seal pups love to play and wrestle with each other, but as they grow up, they begin to spend more and more time alone. Soon, they leave the shore where they were born and take off to explore the world of water.

Sea Lions

Lumbering on Land

Steller sea lions are truly massive animals. Males can weigh almost 2,500 pounds (1,100 kg)—nearly as much as a compact car! These mighty mammals have an appetite to match their size, snacking on everything from salmon to squid. Sometimes, they even steal fish out of nets, much to the displeasure of people fishing.

Steller sea lions are found along the coasts of the North Pacific Ocean from Japan to California, U.S.A. They're known for being chatty, making noises that sound like barks, honks, trumpets, and roars. And since they're social animals that love to gather in groups, the noise can sometimes be deafening.

Sea lion males, called bulls, are several times larger than the females, called cows. Before breeding season arrives, bulls gorge themselves on extra food to bulk up. They arrive at the breeding territory first to stake out an area and get ready to defend it. When the females arrive a few weeks later, a bull will gather up as many females as he can manage into a group called a harem. An adult bull is on high alert during this time, barking, patrolling, and lunging toward rival males. A bull may go for two months without eating while he stays on guard.

When sea lion pups are born, they are already three feet (0.9 m) long and weigh as much as 50 pounds (23 kg). Sea lion mothers use special calls and a keen sense of smell to identify their pups among all the others on the beach.

FROM SKY TO SEA

Some birds don't only fly through the air. These seabirds also "fly" through water, using their wings to dive and paddle below the surface to hunt.

Atlantic Puffins

These bright-beaked birds can dive down 200 feet (61 m) and stay there for up to a minute, eating small fish such as sand eels and herring while underwater.

Common Eiders

These diving ducks inhabit Iceland and other frigid northern places. The feathers they use to insulate their nests, called eiderdown, are so soft and warm that humans collect the leftovers from wild bird nests to fill thick blankets called comforters.

Loons

Named for its awkward, clumsy way of walking on land, loons are agile swimmers that can travel long distances underwater and dive down 200 feet (61 m) with ease. They're known for their unusual cries, which can sound like wails or yodels.

Cormorants

These birds are such fishing experts that humans have looked to them for help. For centuries, fishermen in China and Japan have used trained cormorants that dive beneath the waves, snag fish, and then spit them out in the fishermen's boats.

Wandering Albatrosses

The wandering albatross has the largest wingspan of any bird—up to 11 feet (3.4 m) across! It spends almost its whole life at sea, using shallow dives to catch fish and squid.

Where Rivers Meet the Sea

Water trickles through streams, bubbles through brooks, and roars through rivers, all on its way to flow to the ocean. There, the freshwater mixes with the salty ocean water, forming a new kind of semi-salty, or brackish, water. These places, known as estuaries, are home to a huge host of animals.

Estuaries are constantly changing as the tides move in and out, flooding them or exposing the nutrient-rich, salty mud under the water. And they are protected by landforms such as barrier islands and peninsulas, which shield them from waves, winds, and storms. Many types of habitats are found in and around estuaries, including marshes, mudflats, and mangroves.

As rivers flow into estuaries, they carry in nutrients from the land. Tides also bring in nutrients from the sea. All that food means estuaries teem with life. The Chesapeake Bay of U.S. states Maryland and Virginia, for example, is home to more than 300 species of fish, shellfish, and crab species.

Estuaries are more than just a place for animals to live. The marshy soil and plants there help filter out pollutants to keep the ocean water clean. They also hold onto sediments, preventing shorelines from being washed out to sea. Though many modern cities have been built around estuaries, including New York City and Tokyo, Japan, the development of cities puts estuaries at risk by filling them in to build homes and overfishing their waters.

TYPES OF **ESTUARIES** INCLUDE BAYS, SOUNDS, AND LAGOONS.

THE **CHESAPEAKE BAY** IS THE LARGEST **ESTUARY** IN THE UNITED STATES.

MANGROVES COVER MORE THAN **60 PERCENT** OF TROPICAL SHORELINES WORLDWIDE.

Strong Roots

Most trees can't drink up salty water. But mangroves can. These salt-tolerant trees and shrubs grow on the shores of tropical oceans and are specially adapted to handle their unique environment.

The mud in estuaries can be salty and low in oxygen. Most plants, which absorb oxygen through their roots, can't survive there. But mangroves have exposed roots that absorb oxygen from the air. The plants can also filter salt out of the water to make it usable for the plant. Some excrete salt through glands in their leaves; others concentrate it in their leaves, then shed them.

Mangrove roots trap sediment carried in by rivers, keeping it from being washed out to the ocean. In this way, mangrove forests help the shore from being washed away by waves during tropical storms. Some mangrove forests are protected areas, but more than 35 percent have been cut down to make space for shrimp farms, hotels, and artificial beaches.

Mangrove forests act like nurseries for many ocean creatures, such as rainbow parrotfish and goliath groupers. The tangled network of submerged roots protects the young from larger predators, making these areas perfect places to grow up. Some species, such as Bengal tigers, come to mangrove forests to feed. They roam these forests of the sea, the only tigers that eat crabs and other seafood as an important part of their diet.

THE
ANCESTORS OF TODAY'S
CROCODILES
SURVIVED THE EXTINCTION
EVENT THAT ENDED
THE AGE OF
DINOSAURS.

EPIC REPTILE

It's one of Earth's most fearsome creatures. The largest reptile in the world, the saltwater crocodile can weigh 2,200 pounds (998 kg) and be 23 feet (7 m) long—the length of a dump truck!

The saltwater crocodile can be found mainly in the brackish waters of estuaries in tropical Australia and Southeast Asia. Like all crocodiles, saltwater crocs spend most of their time in the water, coming ashore to warm up in the sun and lay their eggs. They are excellent swimmers and have been spotted swimming 30 miles (48 km) offshore in the open ocean.

Saltwater crocodiles will eat just about anything they can catch, including monkeys, water buffalo, wild boars, and even sharks. While hunting, they lie in wait underwater, holding their breath for up to an hour at a time. When unsuspecting prey wander too close, the croc attacks, using its powerful tail to lunge out of its hiding place at lightning speed. Then, it snaps its jaws shut with incredible force. Saltwater crocs have the strongest bite of any animal ever measured. Scientists believe that they chomp down with about the same amount of force as the mighty *Tyrannosaurus rex* once did.

They may be ferocious predators, but saltwater crocodiles actually make caring parents. After coming ashore to lay a clutch of about 50 eggs, a female croc guards them closely and protects them. When the baby crocs hatch, the mother carries them to the safety of the water in her giant jaws.

FISH OUT OF WATER

These are fish that don't follow the rules. Whenever they choose, these fish can leave their ocean homes behind, flying into the air and flopping—even walking—on land.

Epaulette Sharks

When the tide goes out on the Great Barrier Reef, the epaulette shark doesn't go with it. Instead, it uses its paddle-shaped fins like legs to crawl over the exposed reef. Going from tide pool to tide pool, it hunts for small fish, shrimps, and crabs.

Mudskippers

It's surely one of the strangest fish around. These googly-eyed creatures are called mudskippers, named for their ability to walk, hop, and skip on land. They can breathe through their skin (like frogs) and also trap oxygen-rich water inside their gills—like a scuba diver's tank in reverse! Mudskippers spend their lives mostly out of the sea, slurping up tiny plants and animals that live on muddy shores from West Africa to New Guinea and Australia.

Pacific Leaping Blennies

There's one fish that prefers to be out of the water altogether: the Pacific leaping blenny. Poor swimmers, these fish would be an easy meal in the sea, so they do their best to stay away from the ocean— no easy feat for a creature that has to stay moist to survive! They spend their entire adult lives using their flexible tails to hop from rock to rock, trying to stay in the splash zone without getting sucked under by the waves.

MANGROVE **KILLIFISH** HAVE BEEN FOUND SHELTERING INSIDE OF EMPTY COCONUTS.

Flying Fish

The flying fish speeds underwater at nearly 40 miles an hour (64 km/h), then angles upward. With a flash of scales, it breaks through the water's surface and becomes airborne. Using its large fins to hold it aloft, flying fish can glide 655 feet (200 m)— nearly as long as two football fields end to end!

Mangrove Killifish

You might jump into a swimming pool to cool off. The mangrove rivulus fish, also known as the mangrove killifish, has a different strategy: It jumps out of the water! When the waters of its tropical home get too warm, this fish flips itself end over end, letting the air cool its body. And if drought strikes, the mangrove rivulus can make itself right at home on land, living in crab burrows, hollow logs, and even abandoned soda cans for up to about two months at a time—longer than any other fish.

SEA SLEUTHS

re Columbo nomine Regis Castel
le primum detecta, et ab Amerie
co Vesputio nomen

HIPPOS ARE WHALES' CLOSEST LIVING RELATIVES.

AMBULOCETUS AMBUSHING ITS PREY

The Walking Whale

Whales swim in the sea, spending their lifetimes submerged in water—except for when they leap spectacularly above the waves to the delight of camera-waving whale watchers. But whales, along with seals, sea lions, dolphins, and others, are marine mammals that breathe air and feed their young milk. Why would an air-breathing animal make its home in the ocean?

Whales once had ancestors that lived on land. About 50 million years ago, those creatures began to transition from a life on land to one at sea. Scientists have uncovered fossils that have traits of both land- and ocean-dwellers. One of these "walking whales" is *Ambulocetus* (am-bew-lo-SEAT-us) *natans*, discovered in 1992 in the Pakistan desert, where brackish rivers met shallow seas about 49 million years ago.

Ambulocetus was 11 to 12 feet (3.4–3.7 m) long, weighed about 400 pounds (180 kg), and had lots of sharp teeth. Onshore, it was probably clumsy and slow, pulling itself along with its front limbs like a sea lion. In the water, it swam like a sea otter, propelling itself along using its gigantic hind feet, which were probably webbed. Experts think it might have hunted like a modern crocodile, eating fish and ambushing animals that got too close to the water's edge.

It might not seem like it, but modern whales still hold the evidence of their old walking ways—in their bones. Over millions of years, the front legs of the whale ancestors evolved into flippers. And x-rays show the tiny remnants of hind legs that still grow in the skeletons of some of these enormous sea mammals.

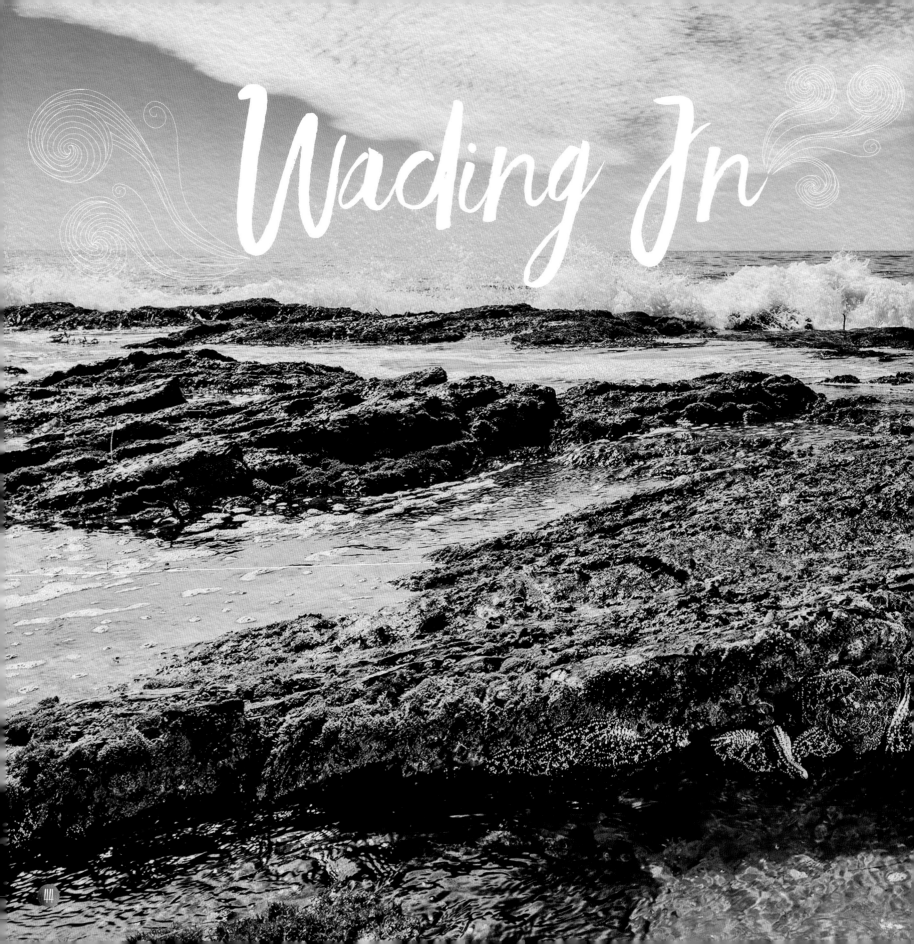

Wading In

The sound of pounding waves fills your ears. You roll up your jeans and step carefully along the rocky shore. The tide is going out, leaving behind glittering pools of water. You bend low, peering into a tide pool. Beneath the water's surface, there is a flurry of activity. Anemones wave their tentacles. Sea stars slowly feel their way around. A shrimp pokes its claw out of a hole in the rock. The shorelines of the world's oceans are bursting with life.

The Snail

To grass, or leaf, or fruit, or wall,
The snail sticks close, nor fears to fall,
As if he grew there, house and all
        Together.

Within that house secure he hides,
When danger imminent betides
Of storm, or other harm besides
        Of weather.

Give but his horns the slightest touch,
His self-collecting power is such,
He shrinks into his house, with much
        Displeasure.

Where'er he dwells, he dwells alone,
Except himself has chattels none,
Well satisfied to be his own
        Whole treasure.

Thus, hermit-like, his life he leads,
Nor partner of his banquet needs,
And if he meets one, only feeds
        The faster.

Who seeks him must be worse than blind,
(He and his house are so combin'd)
If, finding it, he fails to find
        Its master.

—William Cowper

FLAMINGO TONGUE SNAIL

A CONE SNAIL'S **VENOM** TARGETS ITS PREY'S NERVOUS SYSTEM, **PARALYZING IT.**

A Shell-tered Life

Like a tiny tank, a sea snail moves across the ocean floor protected by its hard shell. Famously slow, sea snails get from place to place by crawling with a muscular organ located beneath their bodies. It looks like they are walking on their bellies, and because of this they're called gastropods, which means "stomach foot."

Sea snails live all across the globe, from the Arctic and Antarctic to the tropics. They inhabit all waters, including the deepest ocean trenches, but can most commonly be spotted along the coasts.

Some sea snails are plant-eaters that use a rasping tongue called a radula to scrape algae off rocks. A type of snail called a limpet spends nearly all its time clinging to a rock, with its dome-shaped shell designed to let waves wash over it—without washing it away. Limpets slowly grind their shells into the rock, making a circular groove that fits them perfectly. These circles are the limpet's home, and it will venture only a short distance away to search for algae to eat. If you see a pale, round mark on a coastal rock, you've probably spotted a limpet's house.

Sea snails are slow movers, but that doesn't stop some from hunting down prey! When a cone snail sniffs out food nearby, it shoots a needle-like appendage called a proboscis from its mouth. It injects its prey with venom so potent it can kill worms, fish, and even humans. Brown-and-white cone snail shells are prized by collectors—whose treasure once housed one of the deadliest creatures in the sea!

THE **GIANT TRITON** IS A SEA SNAIL THAT CAN BE 1.5 FEET (0.5 M) LONG.

FINGERNAIL ICE SNAIL

PEOPLE HAVE BEEN USING **CONCH SHELLS** AS TRUMPETS FOR AT LEAST 3,000 YEARS.

NO BONES ABOUT IT

They come in bright colors. They're often covered with spines. And they have an unusual body, with the parts arranged like spokes on a wheel. They're echinoderms, a group of about 7,000 marine creatures that live all over the world.

Sand Dollars

You might have seen one of these pretty white shells with a star shape imprinted on the top washed up on a beach. But this shell is only the creature's skeleton. When alive, sand dollars are purple and covered in bristles. A type of sea urchin, they use their flat bodies to cling close to the sandy seafloor.

Sea Stars

Five-armed sea stars are the most common echinoderms, but there are some species of sea stars with many more arms. The sunflower sea star, for example, begins life with five arms but adds more as it grows. Adults can have as many as 24! The largest sea stars in the world, they can stretch 3.3 feet (1 m) from tip to tip.

Sea Urchins

Urchins use their long spines to keep predators such as crabs and sea otters at bay. On their underside, they have five sharp plates that come together like a beak, which they use to feed on algae and animals such as mussels and sponges.

Sea Cucumbers

They look different from their many-armed cousins, but sea cucumbers are echinoderms just the same. Long and leathery and found on seafloors world-wide, sea cucumbers gather up algae or tiny marine animals with the tentacle-like feet that surround their mouths. When threatened, some perform an unusual defense—they shoot some of their internal organs out of their rear ends! (They later regrow them.)

Feather Stars

Sometimes called "living fossils" because they date back 200 million years, feather stars aren't sea stars but rather a type of echinoderm called a crinoid. Some use their featherlike arms to catch food; others wave their arms rhythmically to swim a short distance.

NUDIBRANCHS ARE MOLLUSKS, JUST LIKE SNAILS AND MUSSELS AND OCTOPUSES AND SQUID. THEY'RE JUST MISSING A **SHELL!**

Nudibranchs

The Rainbow-Colored Slug

When you think of sea slugs, do you think of dull, dreary tubes inching inconspicuously under the waves? Think again! Nudibranchs (NEW-dih-bronks), a type of sea slug, come in a blinding array of brilliant colors and bold patterns. They're one of the most colorful creatures in the ocean.

The nudibranch's extreme colors come from its food. These creatures use a set of curved teeth to munch on corals, sponges, and fish eggs. They absorb the pigments—the substance that gives a creature its color—from their prey, then display them on their outsides. Some nudibranchs also absorb toxic chemicals from their prey, then secrete the poison from their skin. If a predator tries to eat a nudibranch, it will quickly spit out its nasty snack.

There are more than 3,000 known species of nudibranchs in the oceans. There's the Spanish shawl nudibranch, with a deep purple body topped with orange spikes that it uses for breathing. Verco's nudibranch has a neon yellow body covered in bright blue spots. The gas flame nudibranch waves fingerlike projections that are tinted the exact orange and purple colors of a gas flame.

As slugs, nudibranchs may be slow movers—but that doesn't bother one marine hitchhiker. Tiny imperial shrimps like to grab a ride on the back of a Spanish dancer nudibranch as it floats through the water!

Mussels and Their Cousins

From a distance, many of the world's beaches appear to be covered in blue-black rocks. But get closer and you'll realize that they're not rocks at all—they're living creatures! Mussels cluster together in huge groups called beds in many coastal areas. They're bivalves, a group that also includes oysters, scallops, and clams.

There are more than 10,000 species of bivalves, and they live in almost every nook and cranny of the world's oceans, from the warm tropics to the frigid Arctic. Most bivalves can be easily recognized by their shell, which is made up of two halves that are hinged together.

Bivalves are filter feeders: As they cruise through the water searching for their dinner, special gills separate the food from the bits they can't digest, such as sand. In that way, bivalves act like the ocean's water filter—playing an important role of helping keep the water clean. A single oyster can filter more than 50 gallons (189 L) of water in 24 hours!

Bivalves also include some of the longest-living animals known to science: clams. Five-hundred-year-old quahog clams in the North Atlantic Ocean have helped scientists map out the sea's history. That's because clams build their shells in gradual layers, creating rings that can be read to determine Earth's past conditions—just like the rings in a tree's trunk.

MUSSELS HAVE BEARDS. THEY CAN GROW HAIRLIKE FIBERS TO HELP ATTACH THEIR BODIES TO ROCKS.

51

CRUSTACEAN NATION

Shrimps, lobsters, and crabs are the insects of the sea: They have hard outsides called exoskeletons, segmented bodies, and jointed legs. All belong to a group of animals called crustaceans.

Candy Crabs

With its vibrant colors, this crab really does resemble a piece of candy. Also called a soft coral crab, it lives on only one type of coral in the warm waters of the Indian and Pacific Oceans. Its colors vary depending on the shade of the coral where it makes its home, from white to pink to yellow to red.

Remipedes

There are 70,000 species of crustaceans in the world's oceans. But so far, only one has been discovered to be venomous. It's the remipede, a crustacean that looks like a water-dwelling centipede. Two fangs on either side of its head contain venom that paralyzes its victim. Then the remipede digests its prey.

Slipper Lobsters

When they're young, slipper lobsters don't have shells, making them highly vulnerable to predators. So they use a different tactic for defense: invisibility. Young slipper lobsters are almost completely transparent! Experts think their odd eyes might help confuse any predators that do spot them.

Japanese Spider Crabs

The largest known crustacean in the world, the Japanese spider crab can extend 15 feet (4.6 m) from claw to claw and weigh up to 44 pounds (20 kg). That's as much as a medium-size dog! This colossal crawler isn't only the biggest crustacean; it's also the longest living, with some individuals living as long as 100 years.

Pistol Shrimps

Don't mess with this oceangoing quick-draw! The pistol shrimp uses its enormous claw to fire a burst of sound louder than a gunshot. A loud noise by itself may not be deadly, but the speedy snap briefly heats the surrounding water to 8000°F (4427°C) and creates a shock wave that instantly stuns the shrimp's prey of snails, crustaceans, and small fish.

The Myth of Mermaids

Most of our planet is covered by water, so it's little wonder that people once imagined that the deep and mysterious seas could be hiding unfamiliar—even fairy-tale—creatures. Stories of beings that were half human and half fish have existed for thousands of years, in cultures all over the world.

The first mention of mer-people comes from ancient Mesopotamia. There, mermaids were thought to provide protection, and clay figures of them were incorporated into buildings to keep the inhabitants safe. The legendary ancient Greek author Homer wrote about mermaids, too—but his weren't so pleasant. His "sirens" used their enchanting song to lure sailors to wreck their ships on the rocky coast of the sirens' island. In Japan, mermaids took the form of hideous monsters: giant fish with human faces that cursed entire villages with misfortune and hardship if they were captured.

By medieval times, mermaids were so accepted as real creatures that texts showed depictions of them alongside whales and other marine animals. And some sailors were even convinced that they actually saw mermaids at sea. In 1614, a sea captain off the coast of Newfoundland reported that he had spotted a mermaid with large eyes, long green hair, and the body of a fish from the waist down. In 1493, Italian explorer Christopher Columbus wrote about his own mermaid sighting in his ship's log. But he was less than impressed, describing them as "not half as beautiful than they are painted."

Why did Columbus's mermaids look strange? They were actually manatees! In fact, experts think that mermaid sightings through history are actually cases of mistaken identity. Manatees or dugongs are human-size animals with flippers that look a bit like stubby arms and flat, mermaidlike tails. From a distance, it's easy to see how an overexcited oceangoer might have been fooled!

MANATEE

DUGONG

LAND UN

A Y

a tyger

The Citie of
Quinsay
it is a
hundred miles round
The GREAT
ISLE of CIPAN
which some
call JAPAN

The Citie of
CANTON
laden with pepper
and all rich spice

...ia full of
gold &
rich spices

Here also be
Elephants and
Apes

the which

Here do fyshes fly

Here is the

Here is the
his
there is much

TERRA
ANTARCTICA

Here came
Master Christopher
Columbus 1 2

Here be Mermaydens which some do call sirens

THOUGH
MANATEES
ARE SOMETIMES CALLED
SEA COWS,
THEY'RE MORE
CLOSELY RELATED
TO ELEPHANTS.

Reef Life

In the warm, shallow seas of the tropical ocean, rainbow-colored gardens of coral flourish. Sea creatures are everywhere, darting in and out of the reef and hiding in its crevices. There are brilliantly patterned fish, wiggling sea snakes, colorful shrimps, giant manta rays—and countless others besides. Often called the "rainforests of the sea," coral reefs are home to millions of marine species—and scientists estimate there could be millions more just waiting to be discovered. Slip on a snorkel mask or wiggle into a scuba suit and get ready to plunge into an underwater world unlike anything on land.

Amazing Ecosystem

The brilliantly colored corals that make up a tropical reef look like plants. After all, they often have a branching shape, and just as land plants are attached to the ground through their roots, corals are attached to the ocean floor. But corals are animals!

What we call a "coral" is actually a community of hundreds or even thousands of small animals called polyps (PAH-luphs). Polyps have tube-shaped bodies and a crown of tentacles that surround a mouth. They're related to jellyfish and anemones. Like jellyfish, some coral polyps wave their tentacles in the water, stinging any fish and plankton that get too close. Other polyps, however, depend on phytoplankton for their food.

These algae, called zooxanthellae (zo-uh-zan-THEH-lee), actually live inside the coral polyp's body. Like land plants, the algae capture sunlight and turn it into energy in a process called photosynthesis. They use some of this energy for themselves but share most of it—about 90 percent—with their coral polyp host. In return for the food, the coral polyp provides a home for the algae, and also nutrients, plus the carbon dioxide the algae need to grow. Scientists call this kind of partnership, which benefits both creatures, a symbiotic relationship.

A reef begins with tiny polyps that stick to a rock or other hard surface on the seafloor. They grow, and as they do, they form strong skeletons made of limestone. When these coral polyps die, their skeletons remain. New coral polyps land on the skeletons of their ancestors and add their own rocky skeletons. Over time, the coral reef gradually grows. The process is very slow—most reefs grow by less than an inch (2.5 cm) per year. But they're incredibly important to ocean life. Scientists estimate that about one-quarter of all marine species depend on reefs for food and shelter.

SOME OF THE WORLD'S REEFS ARE MORE THAN **45 MILLION** YEARS OLD.

CORALS COME IN ALL SORTS OF SHAPES, FROM DELICATE SEA FANS THAT LOOK LIKE TINY TREES TO ROUND, FOLDED BRAIN CORALS THAT LOOK LIKE, WELL, **BRAINS!**

A World Without Color

Corals are known for their brilliant colors. But all over the world, coral reefs are losing their hues and becoming stark white. This process, known as bleaching, happens because coral polyps are extremely sensitive to changes in their environment.

If the water becomes too warm, the zooxanthellae that live inside the coral polyps will leave, causing the coral to turn white. If the stress is minor, the coral can recover, but if the algae is gone from its coral home for too long, the coral will die. Australia's Great Barrier Reef has lost half its coral since the 1980s.

From 1901 through 2015, the temperature of the sea's surface rose at an average rate of .13°F (.072°C) per decade, and it's continuing to rise due to climate change. That might seem like a small increase, but it's a big deal for sensitive reefs. Some scientists predict that if current global warming continues, most of the planet's reefs will be dead by 2100.

But there is still hope. In 2018, a team of scientists led by U.K. marine biologist James Guest discovered 38 reefs that have managed to escape the damage their neighbors have suffered. Scientists aren't totally sure why these reefs have survived, but they think some might be home to species of coral that can tolerate heat better than others. There's a glimmer of hope that some reefs might be able to adapt to withstand their changing climate and that these rainforests of the sea will survive into the next century.

MORE THAN 500 MILLION PEOPLE DEPEND ON CORAL REEFS FOR FOOD OR INCOME FROM FISHING.

The Inflatable Fish

When most fish sense danger, they dart away to escape. Not the pufferfish. This slow and clumsy swimmer can't speed out of the reach of predators. So it employs a different approach: slurping up so much water that it balloons to several times its size!

Pufferfish, also called blowfish, mostly live in tropical ocean waters. They have round heads and long, tapered bodies—except for when they're puffed up, of course! To achieve this feat, pufferfish fill their highly elastic stomachs with water—or sometimes even air—to turn themselves into living balloons. Some species sport spines on their skin that make them an even less appetizing snack.

If a predator grabs hold of a pufferfish anyway, it's in for an unpleasant surprise. Almost all pufferfish contain a chemical called tetrodotoxin, a substance that makes them foul-tasting at best and lethal at worst. Tetrodotoxin is extremely deadly to humans: Just one pufferfish contains enough to kill 30 adult humans—and there is no known antidote.

Despite the danger, pufferfish meat is considered a delicacy in some cultures. In Japan, it's called fugu, and chefs must be specially trained and licensed to prepare the meat safely. But one slip of the knife can be deadly to diners!

MOST **PUFFERFISH** ARE SMALL, BUT A FEW TYPES CAN GROW UP TO THREE FEET (0.9 M) LONG.

TETRODOTOXIN IS UP TO 1,200 TIMES **MORE POISONOUS** THAN THE DEADLY CHEMICAL CYANIDE.

GIANT MANTA RAYS CAN WEIGH UP TO 5,300 POUNDS (2,400 KG).

Water Wings

Like birds soaring through the sea, giant manta rays flap through the ocean using two triangular fins. These huge creatures can have a 29-foot (8.8-m) wingspan, making them the largest rays in the world. Intelligent and social, giant manta rays gather in groups and are often spotted just off the coasts in warm waters around the world.

Even though giant manta rays are so large, they eat some of the smallest creatures in the ocean: plankton. Rays swim along with their giant mouths wide open, scooping up plankton that they filter through rows of small plates in their mouths. Special paddle-shaped flaps near their mouths help wave more plankton in.

Giant manta rays have the largest brains for their body size of any fish. They have complex social behaviors, such as assembling in a circular formation to feed. Because the ray leading the group gets the most plankton, the rays carefully switch places so each gets a turn in front. They are curious animals that show interest in scuba divers who come to observe them—and there have even been reports of manta rays seeming to approach divers for help in removing fishing line tangled around their fins!

Manta rays often embark on long migrations, traveling hundreds of miles at a time in search of food and finding their way using underwater ocean landmarks. Sightings of giant manta rays are so rare that they remain mysterious animals.

CLOWNFISH **RARELY STRAY** MORE THAN A FEW YARDS FROM THEIR HOST ANEMONE.

CLOWNFISH GET THEIR NAME FROM THEIR BOLD COLORS, WHICH RESEMBLE A **CLOWN'S** FACE PAINT.

REEF BESTIES

Inside an anemone's waving tentacles, there's a flash of color. A striped clownfish (sometimes called an anemonefish) peeks out, checking for danger. Spotting a bigger fish nearby, it darts back, nestling snugly inside the anemone. But anemones are covered with stingers. So why does the clownfish choose this unusual home?

Anemones are stationary animals related to corals and jellyfish. They usually attach themselves to the seafloor or to coral reefs, where they wait for fish to pass close enough to become trapped in their venom-filled tentacles. There are more than 1,000 species of sea anemones found all over the world's oceans, but many live in coastal tropical waters. And a few of them have developed a special relationship with another species: the clownfish.

Brightly colored clownfish would be in trouble without their anemone homes. They are not agile swimmers, making them easy targets for predatory fish such as grouper or barracuda. So the clownfish has come up with a smart safety strategy: It uses an anemone as a shelter. In exchange for a safe place to live, the clownfish cleans the anemone, lets the anemone snack on its leftovers, and chases away predators that feed on anemones, such as butterflyfish.

Clownfish also perform intricate dances, flapping their fins while turning inside the anemone. This wiggle dance isn't just for fun: It circulates the water, moving it around so fresh oxygen is available for the anemone. In return for these services, the anemone does not strike the clownfish, allowing its fish friend to shelter inside its tentacles. On the off chance a tentacle does come in contact with it, the clownfish takes a preventive measure: It slathers itself with a thick layer of mucus from its anemone, which acts like a barrier against stings. Experts call this partnership, which benefits both creatures, a symbiotic relationship. Others might just say the pair is a perfect match!

The Great Barrier Reef

More than 50,000 years ago, a small group of ancient humans landed in Australia for the very first time. They had just completed an incredible journey, traveling all the way across the ocean from Asia with only a crude boat or raft to keep them safe. How these people—perhaps the world's first mariners—accomplished this incredible feat is still a mystery of history.

For many years, these Aboriginal people had Australia to themselves. In that time, they developed complex cultures: more than 200 languages, a hunting and gathering lifestyle, and a rich collection of rituals, dances, and myths. Today, Aboriginal people make up less than three percent of Australia's population. But some of their traditions—including many stories—live on.

Those old stories now have a new life as important scientific evidence. Researchers are cataloging and studying traditional stories to help them piece together a picture of how the continent once was thousands of years ago. Some stories, told by many different groups of Aboriginal people along the northeast coast, tell of a time when the place where the Great Barrier Reef now stands was not covered by water. Their ancestors lived on the flat plains where today fish and corals make their home. But one day, the tales tell, the sea flowed in, and the land was put underwater.

By analyzing details such as geological signs of flooding, scientists are now almost certain that these old stories are no myth—they describe how the coastal area looked thousands of years ago. Changing sea levels flooded the area in shallow water. That provided the perfect conditions for corals, which thrive in warm, sunlit water. Over thousands of years, these creatures collected where the Aboriginal people had once lived, eventually building what is now the largest coral reef system in the world.

THE
GREAT BARRIER
REEF CAN BE
SEEN FROM
SPACE.

REEF FISH

The fish that make their home in a coral reef come in every color of the rainbow. They also sport stripes and spots and many other patterns. There are more than 1,800 species of fish that flap their fins in the coral reefs of Earth's oceans.

Parrotfish

This fish has large teeth that resemble a parrot's beak. Parrotfish use their strong teeth to bite off hard sections of coral to get at the algae that grows there. A second set of teeth in the parrotfish's throat grinds up the coral into small grains— which the fish then expels as sand.

It may be hard to believe, but many of the world's famous white sand beaches are actually made of parrotfish poo!

Surgeonfish

These tropical fish, famous for their wide variety of bright colors from neon yellow to rainbow-striped, get their name from the bladelike spines they sport along the top and bottom of their bodies. Another, venomous spine at the base of their tails helps protect them from predators.

Stonefish

At first glance, it looks like part of the reef. But don't make the mistake of stepping on the stonefish—it's the most venomous fish in the world! Stonefish have rough-textured brown or gray skin splotched with patches of red, orange, or yellow. The 13 spines in its dorsal fin inject venom so toxic it can kill an adult human in less than an hour.

ONE-THIRD OF ALL **SALTWATER FISH** SPECIES LIVE AT LEAST PART OF THEIR LIVES ON CORAL REEFS.

Butterflyfish

These neon-colored swimmers have very thin bodies, which helps them squeeze through small passages so they can reach their favorite foods of coral polyps and algae. Most species wear intricate patterns on bold backgrounds of blue, red, orange, or yellow.

Groupers

Some of the largest residents of the reef, groupers can grow to nearly nine feet (3 m) and weigh more than 882 pounds (400 kg). Some species are grayish or brownish, while others have bright yellow stripes or orange spots. Despite their formidable size, groupers are gentle and will often pose for pictures with scuba divers.

Big Bite

The giant moray eel might look like a snake, but it's actually a long, skinny fish that can grow to 13 feet (4 m)—twice as long as an adult human! Moray eels like to hide in caves and crevices on the reef. They can often be spotted peeking out from their hiding spots.

There are more than 200 species of moray eels that live in tropical seas all over the world. They have a range of sizes, colors, and patterns, but the most familiar is the green moray. This greenish brown creature gets its color from yellowish mucus that covers its blue skin, which helps protect it from parasites and bacteria.

Moray eels have a scary-looking habit of opening and closing their jaws as they rest. This behavior appears fearsome, but it's actually harmless: The eels are just passing water over the gills on the back of their heads to help them breathe.

But that doesn't mean morays are gentle creatures. When a moray spots a tasty-looking fish, it unleashes a fearsome attack. After it grabs the prey in its jaws, it shoots forward a second set of sharp teeth, which bite the victim and pull it down the eel's throat and into its stomach. Moray eels are the only creature on Earth known to hunt this way.

GIANT MORAY EELS LEAVE THEIR HIDING PLACES ON THE REEF AT NIGHT TO HUNT.

Sea Snakes

The Snake That Swims

These snakes don't slither. Instead, sea snakes—which are usually about 3.3 to 5 feet (1–1.5 m) long—spend their lives in the ocean, using their flattened bodies and shortened, paddle-like tails to glide their way through the water.

Though most sea snakes never come on land, they are descended from terrestrial snakes, and so they must still breathe air to survive. Since they also have to dive to the seafloor to eat fish, eels, and fish eggs, sea snakes are usually found in the shallow waters of the Indian and parts of the Pacific Ocean. They have special adaptations that help them survive in their ocean home, such as flaps that close over their nostrils when they're underwater.

Sea snakes can stay submerged for hours at a time—possibly eight or more, experts think. And they're not just good at holding their breath; sea snakes also have a remarkable ability to breathe through their skin. Sea snakes can get about 25 percent of the oxygen their bodies need by absorbing it from the water.

Like some of their land-dwelling relatives, many sea snakes are venomous. The deadliest of them all, the beaked sea snake, has venom more potent than a cobra's or rattlesnake's. But it's very rare that a sea snake bites a human. They are curious and will often come up to divers to inspect them—but they're also gentle and will rarely attack. If they do, their short fangs can't usually bite through a diver's wet suit.

MULTIPLE FISH SOMETIMES LINE UP AT CLEANING STATIONS—**LIKE CARS AT A CAR WASH!**

SEA SCRUB

When you need to clean up, you can wash your hands, shampoo your hair, or scrub off in the shower. But sea creatures have fins and flippers, not hands—not to mention there's no soap on the reef!

So what's a marine animal to do when things get messy? Visit a coral reef cleaning station, of course!

Usually, predators such as large fish, moray eels, and sea turtles will snap up any smaller swimmer that gets too close. But in certain sites on the reef, predator and prey have agreed to a truce. In these special locations, a swimmer in need of a good wash swims up and holds perfectly still, a pose that means "I come in peace." Then, several special cleaner fish swim up.

One species of cleaner fish is a slender fish called a cleaner wrasse. The wrasse carefully inspects the bigger animal's body, picking off and eating bacteria, parasites, and dead skin. The predator will even politely open its mouth so the wrasse can clean between its teeth! In return for this service, the wrasse gets an easy meal. After the bigger fish is spick-and-span, it swims away, leaving the wrasse to work on another visitor. Some animals must love the spa treatment—certain individuals are known to visit more than 100 times a day!

Staying safe while getting up close and personal with dangerous predators takes skill and savvy. Even though wrasses are just four inches (10 cm) long, they are incredibly cunning creatures. Wrasses lure in animals with the promise of removing their parasites—but actually, wrasses often bite off the tasty mucus that coats the animals' skin instead. However, if other clients are watching, they stay on their best behavior and resist the urge to bite. Wrasses also show a remarkable ability to keep track of every visitor to their cleaning stations. That's no small feat: A single wrasse can inspect and clean more than 2,000 sea creatures in one day.

RAINBOW-COLORED ROMANTIC

A rainbow flash scuttles along the seafloor. It's one of the reef's most astounding residents: the peacock mantis shrimp. Brilliant reds, greens, and blues decorate its seven-inch (18-cm)-long, hard-shelled body. But though this beautiful creature looks harmless, watch out! It packs a punch.

This shrimp—actually a creature called a stomatopod that is only distantly related to shrimps—has two secret weapons: clublike front claws that it carries folded beneath its body. When it spots prey, the mantis shrimp springs out one of its claws at incredible speed—50 miles an hour (80 km/h), nearly as fast as a car on the highway! The motion is so quick that it briefly heats up the water around the claw to as hot as the surface of the sun. The hard shells of clams, crabs, and snails are no match for this lightning-fast claw. In fact, the mantis shrimp's punch is so powerful that these animals are rarely kept in aquariums because they can break the glass of their enclosure!

On top of their deadly punch, mantis shrimps boast the most complex eyes in the animal kingdom. Not only can they move independently and see in two different directions at once, they can detect colors that humans are unable to see. While human eyes typically have three types of color-sensing cells (for red, blue, and green, which can be combined to make all the colors of the rainbow), the mantis shrimp has 12 types. Scientists aren't yet sure how the mantis shrimp uses this extraordinary eye power, but it probably helps them hunt.

The life of a mantis shrimp isn't all about hunting down and eating prey. Some species of mantis shrimp are romantics—they choose one partner to share food, shelter, and raise their young with, often staying together for a lifetime. They're the only crustaceans known to do so. Not such a cold-blooded killer after all!

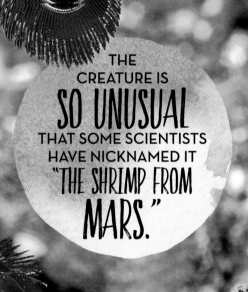

THE CREATURE IS **SO UNUSUAL** THAT SOME SCIENTISTS HAVE NICKNAMED IT **"THE SHRIMP FROM MARS."**

Ocean Forests

Dark and cool, with waving branches and dappled light peeking through: This is a forest, but it's unlike one you've ever experienced on land. Instead of meadows and trees, here there are underwater fields of seagrasses waving gently in the current, and enormous seaweeds as tall as 10-story buildings. In this shady, protected place, all kinds of creatures can be seen through the greenery. Some, like the furry sea otter, are easy to spot. Many others are experts at going unnoticed. But look closely and you'll see all kinds of animals hiding there, from leafy sea dragons that look like part of the landscape to octopuses that can blend into any background.

FOOD OF THE SEA

If you take a walk through a forest on land, you'll see all kinds of life. Birds sing in the branches, a rabbit wiggles its nose in the grass, and insects zip through the air. From the giant redwood forests of California to the rainforests of South America, forests are home to eight out of every 10 land species. The ocean has forests, too: They're known as kelp forests, and just like their cousins on land, they provide a home for many living things.

Kelp looks like a plant, and like plants, it uses the sun's energy to make food through a process called photosynthesis. But kelp is actually a type of algae, a group of water-dwelling organisms that look like plants but lack roots, true stems, or seeds. Algae are often called seaweeds. Some are microscopic, such as phytoplankton, which is the food for all kinds of ocean creatures, from tiny fish to huge whales. There is so much phytoplankton in the ocean that it produces about half the oxygen in the atmosphere.

Other seaweeds are enormous. Giant kelp can grow as tall as 175 feet (53 m)! Since it is not a plant, kelp doesn't attach to the seafloor with roots—instead, it uses a gripping structure called a holdfast. Some species grow air-filled bubbles that help lift their blades toward the sunlight as they grow upward. Giant kelp can grow an astounding two feet (0.6 m) per day.

Kelp prefers cool, coastal waters with lots of sunlight and nutrients. Under the right conditions, kelp can grow into dense underwater forests. Within their branches live all kinds of ocean animals, like eels and spiny lobsters. Sea urchins and snails feast on the kelp's blades, and at the surface, kelp forests are shelters for marine mammals like seals, sea lions, and whales, and birds like great blue herons. Though kelp forests are not as well known as coral reefs, they are nearly as important for ocean life.

SEAWEED IS HIGHLY NUTRITIOUS AND HAS BEEN EATEN IN SOME PARTS OF THE WORLD FOR AT LEAST 1,500 YEARS.

NORRIS'S TOP SNAIL

A Different Kind of Dragon

No, it doesn't breathe fire or do battle with knights. This is another kind of dragon entirely!

Leafy sea dragons are closely related to seahorses, but unlike their cousins, they don't live on tropical reefs, but rather in cooler waters off the southern and eastern coasts of Australia. They have a long, thin snout, which they use like a drinking straw to suck up their favorite food—tiny mysid shrimps—along with other small crustaceans, plankton, and fish larvae. A sea dragon can eat thousands of small creatures every day.

Like seahorses, sea dragons have an unusual arrangement when it comes to reproducing—the males give birth! Female sea dragons deposit their bright pink eggs on the underside of the male's tail. The male carries the eggs until they hatch after four to six weeks, releasing miniature sea dragons into the water.

The leafy sea dragon boasts some of the most fantastic camouflage on the planet. With frilly, leaf-shaped appendages covering its entire body, the leafy sea dragon blends in perfectly with the seaweed it swims among. Because they're hard to spot, little is known about them. But experts do know that the seagrass and seaweed beds where leafy sea dragons live are at risk from threats like pollution. Leafy sea dragons are also often the victims of collectors who want to keep them as pets. Australian law now protects them, in the hopes that these unique dragons of the sea will be around for future generations to marvel at.

THE LEAFY SEA DRAGON'S PLANTLIKE APPENDAGES ARE NOT USED FOR SWIMMING—INSTEAD THIS CREATURE USES TWO NEARLY INVISIBLE FINS TO MOVE.

THE YELLOWLINE **ARROW CRAB** TEARS AND CHEWS UP FRESH SEAWEED TO MAKE IT ROUGH ENOUGH TO STICK TO ITS SHELL.

Decorator Crabs

One Stylish Crab

If you see a bit of the seafloor start scurrying away, stop and take a closer look. You might have spotted a decorator crab, a true expert at camouflage—and one of the only animals on Earth that accessorizes!

Decorator crabs get their name because of their habit of plucking tiny seaweeds and small animals from their environment and sticking them to their shells. Tiny hooked hairs act like

Velcro to hold everything in place. While you might choose your outfit to make a statement, decorator crabs have a different goal: to blend in with their ocean environment so that predators like fish and octopuses can't spot them. Once properly decorated, the crab is extremely hard to see on the ocean floor.

Some decorator crabs are especially choosy about their

shell accessories, selecting items that will not only hide them but will also repel predators, such as toxic seaweed and stinging anemones. Like all crabs, decorators eventually grow too big for their shells and shed, or molt, them. But the crabs don't like to waste their carefully chosen outfits. So when it's time to grow a new shell, they will carefully pluck all their old accessories off the discarded shell and reattach them to the new one. But if the crabs decide to move to a new neighborhood, they'll pluck off their old decorations and choose new ones that better fit in with their new home.

Sea Urchins

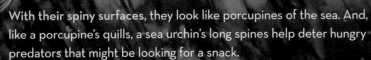
Super Spiny

With their spiny surfaces, they look like porcupines of the sea. And, like a porcupine's quills, a sea urchin's long spines help deter hungry predators that might be looking for a snack.

Sea urchins belong to the same family as sea stars and sand dollars. Underneath their spines, sea urchins have hard bodies like their relatives, but theirs are covered with a spiny shell. Among the spines are hundreds of transparent "tube feet" that the urchins use to scurry their way along the seafloor in search of algae—including kelp—to eat.

But that's not all a sea urchin's tube feet are good for: If a sea urchin gets turned upside down, it can use its tube feet to right itself. If some food falls on top of the urchin, its tube feet become hands that pass the food from one foot to the next all the way to the urchin's mouth. And scientists recently discovered that urchins can see with their feet, too!

Some urchins live in huge groups called hordes. Urchins are voracious eaters, and together, a horde of them can mow down an entire kelp forest. That's become a major problem for the kelp forests off the coast of Northern California. The number of purple sea urchins in the area is exploding, and armies of urchins move through kelp forests, demolishing every scrap of vegetation in their path until there is nothing left. Experts worry that as the kelp forests disappear, the animals that depend on them for food and shelter may disappear, too.

AN **URCHIN'S** TEETH ARE STRONG ENOUGH TO **DRILL THROUGH STEEL.**

Sea Otters

Urchin Eaters

Sea otters are fuzzy and adorable, with a habit of lounging on their backs at the ocean surface like beachgoers soaking up the sun. But much of the time, otters in this pose are not only relaxing—they're also dining on aquatic animals like clams, mussels, crabs, and their very favorite food, sea urchins.

Sea otters gather up shelled creatures, then use a rock they've grabbed from the ocean floor to smash the shells open, revealing the tasty meat inside. With their big appetites, sea otters have traditionally kept the number of sea urchins in check. When otters are around, urchins hide in crevices, surviving on scraps of algae that float by. That keeps the kelp uneaten, allowing it to grow into mighty forests.

But when there aren't enough otters in an area, sea urchins can multiply out of control and destroy the ocean's kelp forests. In that way, kelp forests depend on a healthy population of sea otters to survive.

Once, sea otters were hunted for their luxurious fur coats. Along the California coast, the southern sea otter nearly went extinct. But sea otters are now protected, and today, there are around 125,000 sea otters worldwide. Experts hope that the increasing number of otters will help the sea urchin population get under control. Someday, this conservation success story may in turn help bring back the mighty kelp forests of the California coast.

CREATURES OF THE KELP

More than 1,000 marine species make their home in the kelp forests, where the algae grow as large as trees. Some take shelter in the gently waving canopy of kelp, while others come to hunt.

Bat Rays

Named for their fins that resemble bat wings, bat rays move in from deeper waters toward the shore at night to feed on crustaceans, mollusks, and small fish. Though they have a venomous spine at the base of their tails, bat rays are gentle creatures.

Cabezons

Meaning "big headed" in Spanish, cabezons are large fish that grow up to 2.5 feet (0.8 m) long. They can gulp down anything that fits in their oversize mouths, including squid, prawns, other fish, and even abalones, a type of large sea snail. Cabezons swallow abalones whole, then spit.out the shells.

Leopard Sharks

Common along the coasts of California, leopard sharks are named for the pattern of dark ovals that cover their backs in rows. They often patrol kelp forests, where they skim above the seafloor on the hunt for crabs, clams, fish eggs, and worms.

Kelp Crabs

Colored to match the kelp they climb on, these long-legged crabs spend the summer months grazing on different types of algae, including kelp and sargassum. During winter, kelp crabs change their diet, becoming carnivores that eat mussels and barnacles as well as tiny invertebrates.

California Two-Spot Octopuses

The California two-spot octopus sports glowing blue circles on either side of its head that look like large eyes, perhaps to trick predators into thinking the octopus is a much bigger critter. These octopuses are common aquarium additions—but keepers must be careful, as the creatures are so smart they've been known to escape their tanks!

MORE
THAN 100 SPECIES
OF FISH USE
SARGASSUM
"RAFTS"
AS THEIR
HABITAT.

The Sargasso Sea

REMARKABLE WATERS

It's the most unusual sea on Earth. Located in the North Atlantic Ocean, the Sargasso is the only sea in the world with no shore and no coastlines.

Early explorers were puzzled when they first sailed into the Sargasso Sea. The thick, bright gold plants floating at the surface confused some into thinking land must be nearby. Others were terrified that the fearsome mass was thick enough to trap their ships.

The seaweed that grows in the Sargasso can't drag a ship to a stop—but it is strange indeed. Unlike other types of algae that grow in the world's oceans, the seaweed here, called sargassum, floats freely at the surface, with nothing attaching it to the ocean floor 18,000 feet (5,486 m) below.

Sargassum provides a home to an astounding variety of species. Turtles use it for a nursery, where their hatchlings can have food and shelter. Animals such as white marlins and eels come here to lay their eggs. Porbeagle sharks travel here to give birth to their pups. And many species of shrimp, crab, fish, and other marine creatures found nowhere else on Earth have adapted to live on this floating algae.

Instead of being bordered by land, this sea is encircled by four ocean currents. Together, they form a rotating whirl of water called a gyre that surrounds the sea much like land would. Unfortunately, it's not only ocean creatures that come here—the gyre carries in trash floating in the ocean. Billions of bits of plastic are trapped in the Sargasso Sea by the currents, in some places more than 520,000 bits per square mile (200,000 bits per square km). The garbage patch stretches across the entire Sargasso Sea, an area roughly the distance from Cuba to the U.S. state of Virginia.

SEA SLEUTHS

DEPENDING ON THE SPECIES OF PLANKTON, RED TIDES CAN TURN COASTAL WATERS NOT ONLY RED, BUT ALSO **ORANGE, BROWN, PINK, OR YELLOW.**

Forecasting the Red Tide

Most of the time, algae are harmless plants that feed a huge variety of ocean creatures. But sometimes, dangerous kinds of algae can grow out of control. These harmful algal blooms, or HABs, can produce toxins that have damaging effects on animals or people—and on entire ecosystems.

Normally, all the organisms within an ecosystem exist in a balance. But as with the sea urchins and sea otters (see p. 84), sometimes the balance gets out of whack. HABs happen when algae grow rapidly in dense patches on the ocean's surface—often referred to as "red tides" because they make the water appear red. They can become so dense that they clog up harbors, cover up corals, or block the sunlight that seagrasses and other marine life need to survive.

HABs seem to be happening more often—and are getting bigger. Scientists think this may be due to polluted runoff (water that washes from land out to sea) and the warming climate, which might be making it easier for some kinds of algae to grow. The growing algae can use up all the oxygen in the water, causing marine life to leave the area or die. It can also produce toxins that make shellfish harmful to eat and can also contribute to the deaths of animals like manatees and sea lions. These toxins can also get into the air, where they make vacationers and people who live on the coast sick.

Scientists are hard at work studying why HABs happen and how to predict when they will occur. Some researchers are experimenting with a sensor that can identify when dangerous species of algae are in the area and alert people to their presence. Others have developed a forecasting system that uses satellite imagery and information about water conditions to predict how blooms will spread. At the same time, they're studying the causes of the blooms to try to prevent them—and keep the red tide from washing ashore in the future.

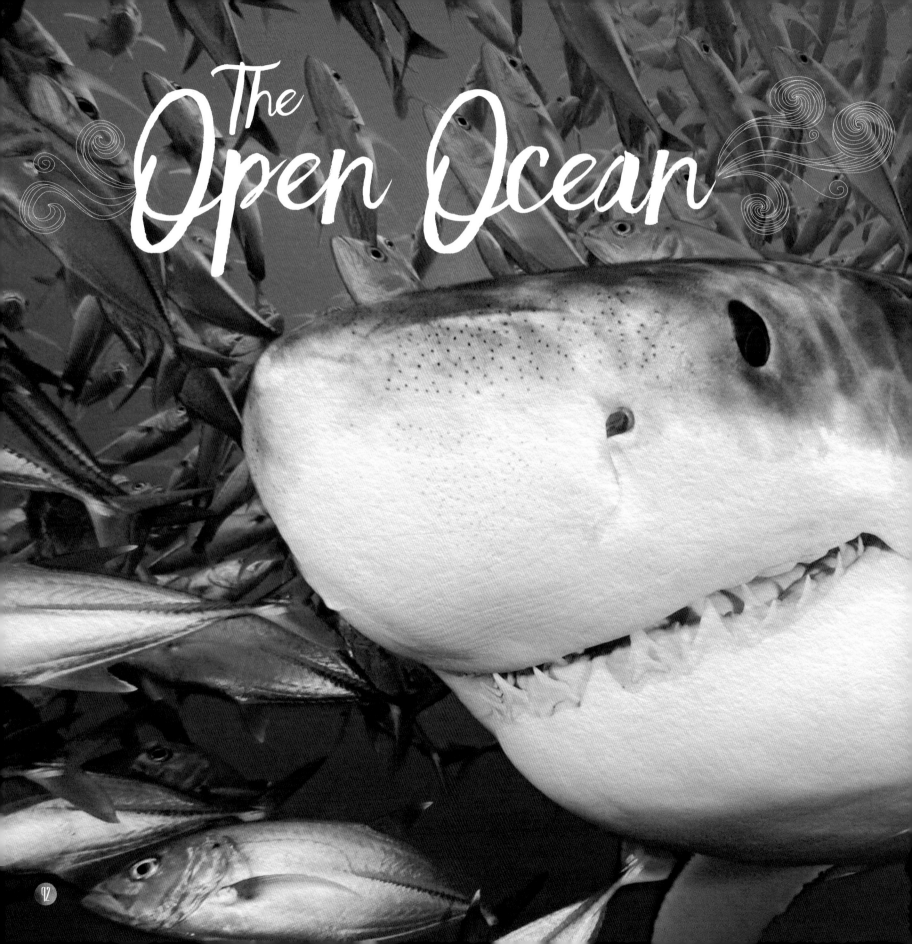

The Open Ocean

To enter the open ocean is to dive into a world where water stretches in every direction as far as the eye can see. More than 70 percent of Earth's surface is covered by water, most of it more than two miles (3.2 km) deep. This part of the sea teems with life, from delicate jellies that float on the currents to anchovies that swirl in enormous schools. Many creatures of the open ocean go their entire lives without ever touching the shore, the seafloor, or the surface—or even knowing they exist. For them, it's a watery world.

THE BIGGEST ANIMAL EVER

The mighty blue whale, with a tongue that weighs as much as an elephant and a heart as heavy as a car, isn't only the largest animal on Earth; it is also the biggest creature there has ever been. Blue whales, which rule nearly all the world's oceans, can be up to 100 feet (30 m) long and weigh 200 tons (181 t)—more than twice as long as a school bus and 16 times as heavy!

A blue whale reaches its massive size on a diet of surprisingly small creatures: tiny shrimp-like animals called krill. It must eat a huge amount of krill to survive—four tons (3.6 t) a day during certain times of the year. To do this, the whale uses baleen, coarse bristles in its mouth that look like the teeth of a comb hanging down from the whale's upper jaw. Baleen is made from the same material as human hair. The whale gulps up a huge mouthful of water, then uses its giant tongue to force the water out through the thin, overlapping baleen plates. Thousands of krill are left behind and swallowed.

Blue whales have a voice to match their size: They're thought to be some of the loudest animals on Earth. Their pulses, groans, and moans transmit vast distances through the ocean, carrying their calls up to 1,000 miles (1,609 km). Blue whales use these vocalizations to communicate with other whales and to navigate the ocean depths, by listening for their echoes off undersea objects.

In the 1900s, blue whales were hunted almost to extinction for their oil, which was used as fuel for lamps and to make soap. About 360,000 of these giant creatures were killed between 1900 and the mid-1960s before they were finally protected by international law. They are still at risk: Experts estimate there may be as few as 10,000 of these giants of the sea left on the planet.

THE SPRAY FROM A **BLUE WHALE'S** BLOWHOLE CAN SHOOT NEARLY 30 FEET (9 M) INTO THE AIR.

WITH AN AVERAGE ESTIMATED LIFE SPAN OF AROUND **80 TO 90 YEARS,** BLUE WHALES ARE AMONG SOME OF THE LONGEST-LIVED ANIMALS ON EARTH.

TINY BUT MIGHTY

Scoop up a jar of ocean water and peer inside: What do you see? It might look like there's nothing there, but that's far from the truth. Billions of miniature creatures drift with the ocean's currents and are the basis of all marine life. They're plankton.

Some, called phytoplankton, are plantlike. Similar to land plants, they use photosynthesis to produce energy from sunlight, carbon dioxide, and water, releasing oxygen in the process. There are many types of phytoplankton, including dinoflagellates and diatoms. Dinoflagellates use a whiplike tail to move through the water. Diatoms have rigid shells and no way to move through the water, so they rely on ocean currents to travel. Another type of phytoplankton is *Prochlorococcus*. They live about 328 feet (100 m)—about the length of a football field—below the surface and are so tiny that 40 of them could fit in a line across the width of a human hair. They are so small that they went undiscovered until the 1980s. Now scientists think there are more of them than any other photosynthetic organism on Earth.

Other plankton, called zooplankton, are animal-like. Some are tiny wormlike creatures called arrow worms, which use rows of sharp teeth to deliver venom that can bring down smaller creatures. Some are copepods, small crustaceans that use paddle-like appendages to swim. And others are shrimplike krill.

Zooplankton feed on phytoplankton, and in turn they become food for larger ocean creatures such as fish and giant blue whales (see p. 94). Plankton is such an important food source that ocean life could not exist without it.

SCIENTISTS ESTIMATE THAT PLANTLIKE **PHYTOPLANKTON** PRODUCE BETWEEN 50 AND 80 PERCENT OF THE PLANET'S OXYGEN.

SMALL SNACK, BIG EATERS

Some of the ocean's biggest animals eat the tiniest food: plankton. Plankton-eaters include the mighty blue whale, the enormous whale shark, the giant bowhead whale, and an unusual creature called the megamouth shark. This 16-foot (5-m)-long animal can have a mouth about four feet (1.3 m) across! Scientists think that megamouth sharks spend most of their lives in the dark of the deep ocean, only coming near the surface at night to feed. Though scientists know the shark uses its huge mouth to filter plankton out of the water, they're not sure of the details because no one has ever witnessed this mysterious creature feeding.

MEGAMOUTH SHARK

NO BRAIN, NO PROBLEM

Jellyfish have no brains, no blood, and no bones, and only the most basic of sense organs. Yet they have been drifting along on the ocean's currents for hundreds of millions of years—essentially unchanged since before dinosaurs roamed Earth.

Black Sea Nettles

This deep red creature is a giant among jellyfish: Its bell-shaped body can be three feet (0.9 m) across and its tentacles 25 feet (7.6 m) long or more. The jelly is often seen in the company of butterfish, which hide inside it when threatened.

Moon Jellies

Named for their translucent circular bodies, these jellies can be found worldwide. Because they're see-through, their food—such as orange brine shrimps—is visible inside them.

Box Jellies

It's one of the most toxic animals on Earth. The box jelly's extremely powerful venom kills prey instantly, so there is no struggle to escape, which could damage the jelly's delicate tentacles. Strangely, sea turtles aren't affected by the venom, and these jellies are one of their favorite snacks.

JELLYFISH HAVE LIVED IN EARTH'S OCEAN FOR MORE THAN **500 MILLION YEARS.**

THE JELLY THAT ISN'T

The Portuguese man-of-war is an ocean drifter that may look like a jellyfish, but it's not. In fact, it's not even a single creature. It is a group of four organisms called polyps working cooperatively to form one bigger critter. One of the polyps is a gas-filled bubble that keeps the creature floating along the sea surface. The second holds its digestive organs; the third its reproductive organs. And the fourth forms the man-of-war's tentacles, which can extend 165 feet (50 m) and are venomous.

PORTUGUESE MAN-OF-WAR

Egg-Yolk Jellies

This creature looks like a big egg cracked and poured into the water, with hundreds of tentacles surrounding its yolk-yellow center. Crabs and other small critters have been found hitching a ride inside these jellies.

SWIM TEAM

The ocean can be a dangerous place, full of fast-moving predators on the hunt for their next meal. That's why some fish choose not to go it alone: Instead, they swim together in groups called schools. Some have only a few members; others can contain hundreds of thousands or even millions of fish, making them the biggest gatherings of animals on the planet.

Schooling fish come together for protection. Forming a massive, tightly compacted group makes it difficult for a predator to pick out only one individual to attack. The swirling mass of fish confuses and overwhelms hunters, keeping fish in a school much safer than those that swim alone. Fish that school include species such as anchovies, herring, and sardines.

Schooling fish move in mesmerizing patterns, darting and changing direction all at once, as if they are a single, much larger creature. Each individual closely watches its neighbors in the school. If the fish behind gets too close, it will speed up, and if the fish in front gets too close, it will slow down. To keep such good track of its neighbors and move in the blink of an eye, the fish uses visual cues, as well as an organ along each side of its body called the lateral line, which can sense even the smallest pressure changes in the water.

But the details of schooling behavior are still mostly a mystery to science. Unlike groups of many other animals, such as horses, schools of fish do not have leaders. No one fish is making decisions for the group to follow—so how do they decide when and where to move?

SCIENTISTS ARE STUDYING SCHOOLING BEHAVIOR IN THE HOPE OF DESIGNING DRONES THAT COULD ORGANIZE THEMSELVES TO ACCOMPLISH A TASK, SUCH AS MONITORING FOREST FIRES.

MANY FISH SCHOOL AT SOME POINT IN THEIR LIFE CYCLE—OFTEN WHEN THEY ARE YOUNG.

BLUEFIN TREVALLIES

CUTTLEFISH
ARE MEMBERS OF THE
MOLLUSK FAMILY,
THE GROUP THAT
INCLUDES SNAILS,
SQUID, AND
MUSSELS.

SCIENTISTS
PUT A BLACK-AND-WHITE
CHECKERBOARD
INSIDE CUTTLEFISH TANKS.
THE CUTTLEFISH
WERE ABLE TO MIMIC
THE PATTERN!

Cuttlefish

QUICK-CHANGE ARTISTS

Despite their name, cuttlefish aren't fish at all: They belong to a group of sea creatures called cephalopods, some of the strangest—and smartest—animals in the ocean.

Along with their octopus and squid cousins, cuttlefish have an amazing ability to change their skin's pattern, color, and texture. They use this trick to blend in with their surroundings, disguising themselves perfectly among rocks or coral. This camouflage helps them evade predators, stealthily hunt their prey, and even communicate.

When predators come along, a cuttlefish can make two dark spots appear on its back that look like the eyes of a much bigger creature. That's enough to scare off any attacker! When hunting, cuttlefish use special color-changing cells in their skin to flash in a mesmerizing color show. The display lures in prey animals such as small fish and puts them into a trance. Then the cuttlefish strikes! Dinnertime.

But perhaps the most incredible way a cuttlefish uses its ability to change its appearance is to fool other cuttlefish. A male mourning cuttlefish will flash a pattern of bold zebra stripes to show off for a female. But if a competing male swims by, the first male will play a trick: He'll keep the zebra pattern only on the side of his body facing the female. On the other side, facing the rival male, he'll change his pattern to a spotty brown that mimics the skin of a female. That fools the rival into thinking he's not competition. "Nothing to see here!" he says. Now that's sneaky!

Hunter or Hunted?

The largest predatory fish on Earth, great white sharks can grow longer than 20 feet (6 m) and weigh up to 5,000 pounds (2,268 kg)—bigger than an SUV!

Great whites are powerful swimmers. With bodies shaped like torpedoes, they slide through the water, using their powerful tails to propel them forward at speeds of up to 15 miles an hour (24 km/h). They are such strong swimmers that they can even leap all the way out of the water as they attack their prey from underneath, taking the hapless critter by surprise.

These sharks are exceptionally well-adapted for finding and catching prey, with mouths lined with as many as 300 serrated (jagged) teeth in several rows. They have such an acute sense of smell that they can detect one drop of blood in 25 gallons (95 L) of water. And they even have a sixth sense: the ability to detect tiny electromagnetic fields generated by animals underwater. Their prey, including sea lions, seals, and small toothed whales, are usually no match for great whites.

Though great whites are indeed apex predators (meaning they are at the top of their food web), their threat to humans is often exaggerated. Fatal shark attacks are extremely rare—statistically, a person is more likely to be killed by fireworks! The reality is that sharks are in much greater danger from humans than humans are from sharks. About 100 million sharks of all species are killed by humans every year, and great whites—though they are such formidable creatures—are considered a vulnerable species.

SHARKS DO NOT HAVE TRUE BONES. INSTEAD, THEIR SKELETON IS MADE OF CARTILAGE—THE SAME STUFF THAT FORMS YOUR EARS AND NOSE.

EACH **DOLPHIN** HAS ITS OWN PERSONAL WHISTLE THAT OTHER DOLPHINS USE TO IDENTIFY IT— LIKE A HUMAN'S NAME.

Bottlenose Dolphins

Smart Swimmer

They have permanent smiling expressions and playful natures—and even seem to enjoy surfing waves! They're also extremely intelligent: Dolphins are thought to be some of the smartest animals on the planet—perhaps even smarter than chimpanzees and gorillas.

Dolphins can be trained to perform all kinds of tricks, such as corkscrewing out of the water and standing upright on their tails. Scientists suspect that dolphins probably developed their intelligence because they live in complex social groups—just like humans. They travel in groups called pods that are made up of around 10 to 15 members. They cooperate to play, hunt, and raise young dolphins.

To work together, dolphins must communicate—and they're some of the most talkative creatures in the sea. Dolphins click, squeak, and squawk. They use body language, too, leaping as high as 20 feet (6 m) into the air, snapping their jaws, and blowing bubbles.

Dolphins are skillful hunters. They track their prey using echolocation—sending out up to 1,000 clicking noises per second, then listening for those clicks to bounce off objects and back to the dolphins' ears. Using this method, they can tell the location, size, and shape of their target—even in dark or murky water. Dolphins will work together to hunt, sometimes herding fish into circles or corralling them inside rings of stirred-up mud for easy eating.

LIFE IN THE OPEN OCEAN

More than 90 percent of the livable space on Earth is in the open ocean. It's no wonder that this area, also called the pelagic zone, is home to endless varieties of fish.

Ocean Sunfish

The world's largest bony fish, the ocean sunfish, or mola mola, can grow to 11 feet (3.4 m) and weigh up to 2.5 tons (2.3 t). They're clumsy swimmers that waggle their fins to move and can never fully close their mouths, giving them a permanently surprised expression.

Bristlemouth Fish

This is not only the most abundant fish on Earth, it's also the most numerous of all vertebrates (animals with a backbone): the bristlemouth, smaller than a fingertip with a mouthful of needle-like fangs. Scientists estimate there could be quadrillions, or thousands of trillions, of them—at least five times more than there are stars in the Milky Way.

Oceanic Whitetip Sharks

Top predator of the tropical open oceans, the oceanic whitetip shark feeds on bony fishes, squid, turtles, stingrays, and even seabirds. Sadly, populations in some areas have dropped by 90 percent, as they are often hunted for their fins, which are used to make a traditional Chinese dish called shark fin soup.

Mackerel

Mackerel use their torpedo-shaped bodies to speed through the water in search of food such as plankton, crustaceans, and fish eggs. During the spring and early summer, they come together in schools to spawn, or release their eggs, in the upper part of the water. During the winter, they descend to the ocean's depths.

Swordfish

Swordfish are some of the fastest fish in the sea. Their long bills help them cut through the water, and their bodies are aerodynamic, allowing them to reach speeds of up to 75 miles an hour (120 km/h).

SEA SLEUTHS

The Search for Longitude

In the 18th century, navigating the open ocean was incredibly dangerous. Sailors had long used the position of the sun or the North Star (the brightest star in the Little Dipper constellation) to figure out their latitude—in other words, their distance north or south of the Equator. But they had no way to accurately calculate longitude, or their distance from a north–south dividing line called the Prime Meridian.

Many oceangoing disasters occurred as a result. In 1707, a British naval fleet's navigational miscalculation caused four ships to crash into the rocks surrounding the Isles of Scilly off the coast of England, killing more than 1,300 sailors. It was one of the British Navy's greatest tragedies of all time. To try to prevent future losses, the British government offered a £20,000 reward—several million dollars in today's currency—to anyone who could come up with a way to calculate longitude at sea.

In 1728, a man named John Harrison took up the challenge. A self-taught carpenter and clockmaker, Harrison set his mind on coming up with a solution. He knew that since Earth rotates 360 degrees in 24 hours, it rotates 15 degrees each hour. If sailors at sea knew the time in their current location and also the time at the Prime Meridian, the location of 0° longitude, they should be able to calculate their longitude. The problem was creating a clock that could keep time accurately at sea, where the rocking of the waves, changing temperatures, and exposure to storms usually threw off a clock's mechanism.

It took about 40 years of work, but Harrison eventually came up with the chronometer, a timepiece that could be used to accurately calculate longitude on open ocean voyages. Explorers such as Captain James Cook, who mapped the Pacific, New Zealand, and Australia, did so with the help of Harrison's device. Chronometers remained vital tools for seafarers until GPS satellite became widely available around the year 2000.

On the Move

The sea is vast. The Pacific Ocean alone covers about one-third of Earth's surface, more than all the planet's land combined. At its greatest width, it stretches more than 12,000 miles (19,300 km)—halfway around the world. Yet even this distance is not too much for some oceangoing travelers. These residents of the open ocean journey thousands of miles per year across Earth's waters in pursuit of food or breeding grounds. They're some of the most incredible swimmers in the sea.

HOMEWARD BOUND

Every four years, millions of sockeye salmon begin an epic journey. They make their way thousands of miles from the Pacific Ocean back to the freshwater streams, rivers, and lakes where they were born. To do it, they must travel upstream, swimming tirelessly against the current and even leaping high out of the water to make it over waterfalls. The entire journey may take these fish more than a year.

When the salmon arrive at last at the spawning grounds of their birth, they perform their final act. The female salmon digs a nest with her tail and pushes thousands of eggs inside for the male to fertilize. After this, the salmon die. It's time for the next generation to take to the water.

About one month later, young salmon, called alevins, hatch. They are tiny with enormous eyes, and their bodies are attached to bright orange food sacs a bit like egg yolks. After a few weeks, the alevins have grown bigger and stronger. They emerge from the nest, then spend the next few years eating and growing, until at last they are strong enough to make their own journey out to sea where there are many more food sources to sustain them as adult salmon. On their way, their bodies undergo a complex internal change that allows them to survive in salt water instead of fresh.

The salmon live in the sea for one to four years, until they are old enough to reproduce. Then it's time to return to their freshwater birthplace. Precisely how the salmon are able to undertake this complex journey—how they navigate to the coast, to the correct river, and upstream, making the right choice at every fork in their path to eventually arrive at the exact place they were born—is still a mystery. Scientists think salmon use many tools, such as Earth's magnetic field and their sense of smell, to navigate in one of the greatest migration feats of the animal kingdom.

SOCKEYE SALMON GET THEIR **BRIGHT** ORANGE COLOR FROM THE KRILL THEY EAT.

OCEAN HUNTERS

These predators of the open ocean are fast swimmers and agile hunters—and they're hungry for their next meal. It takes a lot of food to feed their large bodies, so these hunters travel great distances across the seas in search of prey.

Pacific Bluefin Tuna

Just after their first birthday, Pacific bluefin tuna embark on a long-distance journey, traveling 5,000 miles (8,000 km) from their spawning grounds in the Sea of Japan to the California coast, where food is plentiful. To do it, they swim through icy waters in the Arctic that hover near the freezing point. Special adaptations allow them to retain heat as they swim, making them one of the few warm-blooded fish in the sea.

Sailfish

Some of the the fastest fish in the sea, sailfish can reach speeds of up to 68 miles an hour (109 km/h) when in pursuit of prey. Following ocean currents, they travel more than 2,237 miles (3,600 km) to find food. When hunting, sailfish fold their fins back so they can move quickly, then strike with their bills to stun or kill. They most often eat schooling fish such as mackerel, sardines, and anchovies.

White Marlins

Sleek and powerful, the white marlin has a body designed for long-distance swimming. Growing to be as long as nine feet (2.7 m) and weighing 180 pounds (82 kg), they live in the open waters of the tropical and temperate Atlantic, migrating from a summer habitat in the northern Gulf of Mexico, where they spawn, to winter grounds in the southern Caribbean.

Elephant Seals

Every spring, massive elephant seals leave the beaches of Mexico and southern California and slip into the cool Pacific. After three months of going hungry during the birthing and breeding season, they're ready to eat—but to do it, they must swim to their foraging grounds in the North Pacific to feast on prey such as squid and shark. Their two annual migrations cover as much as 13,000 miles (21,000 km).

Shortfin Mako Sharks

These sharks are superfast swimmers, exhibiting bursts of speed up to 35 miles an hour (56 km/h). That makes them the world's fastest sharks, and astounding migrators known to travel more than 1,300 miles (2,092 km) in a little over a month. Scientists are still learning exactly where and why these sharks migrate, by tagging them with electronic trackers and observing their travel patterns.

LEATHERBACKS CAN DIVE DEEPER THAN ANY OTHER TURTLE, WITH THE **DEEPEST RECORDED DIVE** REACHING MORE THAN 4,000 FEET (1,200 M).

OCEAN VOYAGERS

The largest turtles on Earth, leatherbacks can grow up to seven feet (2.1 m)—longer than an adult human is tall! And they can exceed 2,000 pounds (907 kg)—the weight of a large horse. Unlike other sea turtles, which have hard, bony shells, leatherbacks have an inky blue shell that is rubbery and flexible. These huge reptiles are truly ancient: They've roamed the seas for 100 million years—meaning this species lived on Earth at the same time as the dinosaurs.

Leatherback sea turtles undertake one of Earth's greatest migrations, the longest of any sea turtle. In search of jellyfish to eat, they can travel 10,000 miles (16,093 km) or more each year, crossing the entire Pacific Ocean as they travel from Asia to the West Coast of the United States. Then they reverse direction to their nesting areas to breed, sometimes on the very beach where they were born. How the turtles are able to navigate across vast oceans to return to the place they emerged from their eggs is one of the great mysteries of ocean science. When females are ready, they dig a hole in the sand under the cover of darkness and lay about 80 eggs. Then they fill the hole back up with sand before returning to the sea.

Only about one in 1,000 leatherback hatchlings makes it out of the nest, to the sea, and all the way to adulthood successfully. And survival is only getting tougher for these sea travelers. Leatherbacks are at risk as their nesting habitats are destroyed by human intrusion and development. They are also vulnerable to becoming entangled in fishing lines or nets and being struck by boats. They can die if they accidentally eat plastic that they've mistaken for their favorite food—jellyfish. Once found swimming in all ocean waters except in the Arctic and Antarctic regions, leatherbacks are now in rapid decline in many parts of the world.

MIGHTY MOVERS

Humpback whales are truly enormous animals. Stretching up to about eight times as long as a twin bed, they sport 16-foot (4.9-m) flippers and 18-foot (5.5-m) tails. They also undertake some of the most monumental migrations on the planet, roaming all over the world's seas with the changing of the seasons.

Humpback whales migrate farther than any other mammal on Earth. During the summer, many humpbacks spend their time feeding on krill, plankton, and small fish in the rich waters of the polar oceans. When winter comes, they migrate to warm tropical oceans, where they mate and give birth to their calves. Humpbacks regularly travel about 3,000 miles (4,800 km) between their breeding and feeding grounds. One humpback was even recorded taking a round trip between American Samoa and the Antarctic Peninsula—11,706 miles (18,840 km)!

From 2003 to 2010, scientists monitored 16 whales tagged with satellite trackers as they migrated. They found that the whales took incredibly straight routes to their destinations, never moving more than about five degrees off course. How they stick to such an arrow-straight path, especially in an ocean of endless blue in every direction, is a marvel. Scientists don't yet understand the feat, but they think humpbacks probably navigate using Earth's magnetic fields and the position of the sun, moon, and stars.

Experts think there may be something else humpbacks use to navigate: their songs. Humpback whales are famous for their haunting, beautiful calls that can carry hundreds or even thousands of miles underwater. Humpbacks sing intricate melodies of moans, howls, and cries that scientists suspect they use to communicate. Perhaps one thing the whales are singing about is their underwater position and route. This would help migrating whales coordinate their movements as they swim on their long-distance journeys around the world.

THE HUMPBACK WHALE'S SONG IS AMONG THE MOST COMPLEX IN THE ANIMAL KINGDOM.

HUMPBACK WHALES USE THEIR MASSIVE TAIL FINS TO PROPEL THEMSELVES COMPLETELY OUT OF THE WATER IN A LEAP CALLED A BREACH.

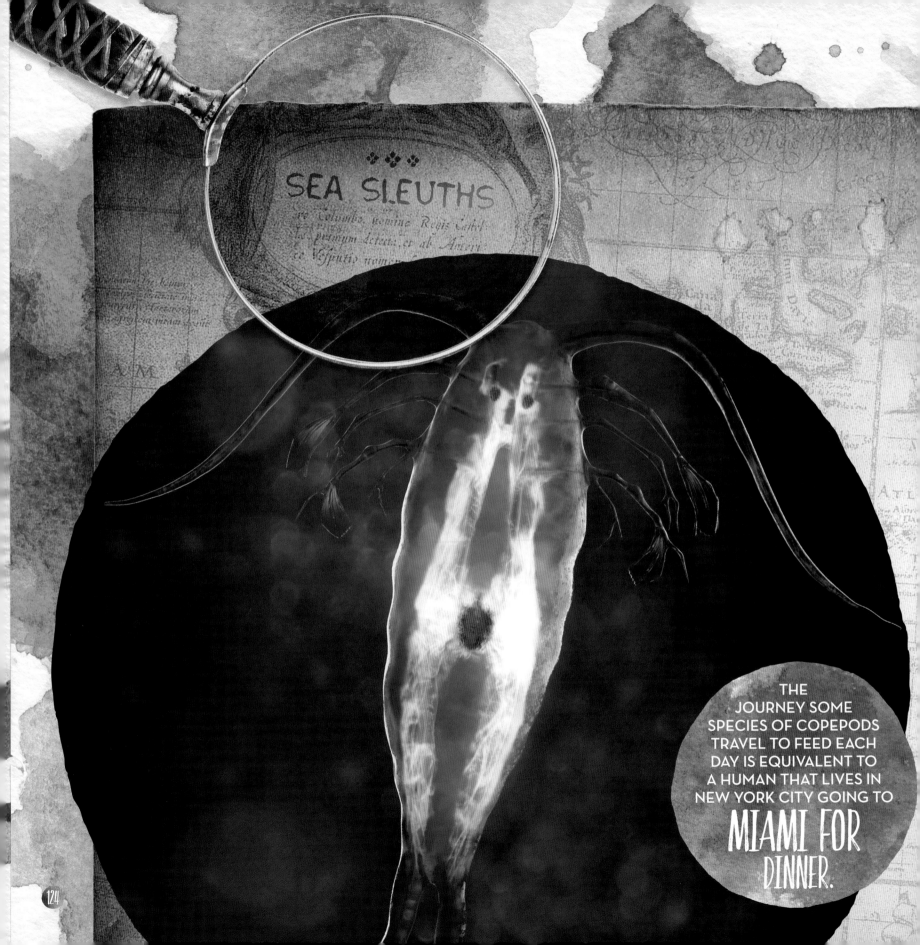

SEA SLEUTHS

THE JOURNEY SOME SPECIES OF COPEPODS TRAVEL TO FEED EACH DAY IS EQUIVALENT TO A HUMAN THAT LIVES IN NEW YORK CITY GOING TO MIAMI FOR DINNER.

Migration Mysteries

It's Earth's largest wildlife migration—and it occurs every day. But because it happens out of sight of humans, we are only beginning to learn its secrets.

As night darkens the sky, huge numbers of ocean creatures make their way out of the depths and rise toward the surface. They include small crustaceans called copepods, shrimps, krill, jellyfish, squid, and many more. All together, about 5.5 billion tons (5 billion t) of animals move upward each night, then sink back down when the sun comes up.

This up-and-down pattern is called diel vertical migration ("diel" means "day") and it happens all over the world, in both salt water and freshwater. The upper layers of the water are home to microscopic algae and other tiny plants that flourish in the sunlight there. The swimmers come to the surface to snack on this buffet, but they do it only under the cover of darkness, when it's harder for predators to find them. Before the sun comes up, they retreat down to the dark safety of the deep.

It wasn't until the 1940s that scientists got their first hints that this mass migration was occurring right under our noses, and much about it still remains a mystery. Because the deep ocean is still mostly unexplored, scientists are only beginning to understand this nightly dance.

So far, they've learned that diel vertical migration includes a fantastic variety of organisms, from wiggling comb jellies to whiplike snipe eels to glowing lanternfish. Some travel only a few dozen feet in a night, whereas others can venture several thousand. And, incredibly, vertical migration happens even during winters in the North Pole, when the sun never rises at all. There, tiny migrators move in rhythm with the moon, sinking to the deep sea to avoid the faint light it casts on the ocean surface. As scientists continue to explore, they'll slowly uncover more secrets of this hidden ocean migration.

Life on the Icy Edge

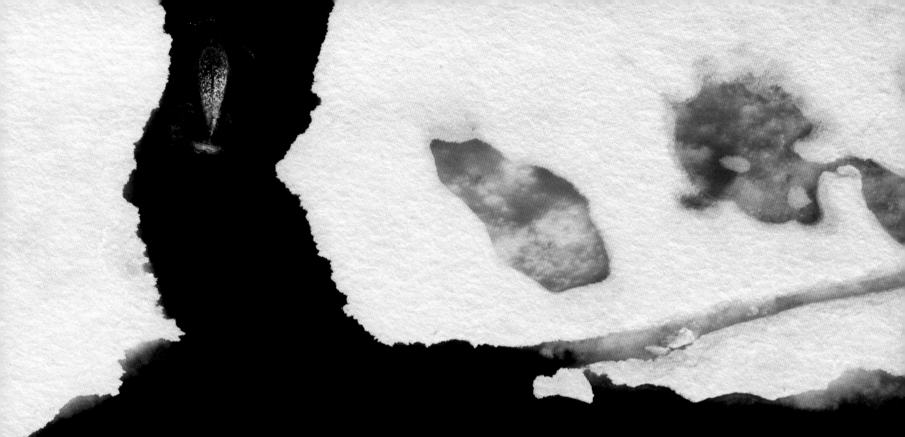

Beyond the warm waters of the Equator, through wide stretches of open ocean, farther and farther still are the very ends of the Earth. Here, waves lap against shores made of pure white ice. At its coldest, the water here in the polar oceans can be a frosty 28°F (-2°C). On shore, conditions are even harsher, with frigid winds, howling storms, and nothing but ice and snow in every direction. Yet the ocean waters around the Arctic and Antarctic are rich with life. They bloom with phytoplankton. Those in turn attract huge schools of zooplankton, fish, pods of migrating whales, seal and sea lion colonies, and many other animals.

A Penguin

THE Pen-guin sits up-on the shore
And loves the lit-tle fish to bore;
He has one en-er-vat-ing joke
That would a very Saint pro-voke:
"The Pen-guin's might-i-er than the
Sword-fish";
He tells this dai-ly to the bored fish,
Un-til they are so weak, they float
With-out re-sis-tance down his throat.

—Oliver Herford

128

Cold-Weather Experts

Humans could not survive unprotected on the Antarctic ice, where windchills can drop the temperature down to minus 76°F (-60°C). But it's home sweet home for one of Earth's toughest species: the emperor penguin. The largest of all penguins, emperors stand about 45 inches (114 cm) tall—about the height of a second grader! These birds spend their entire lives on the Antarctic ice and in its waters, using a host of clever adaptations and behaviors to make it in their harsh home.

EMPEROR PENGUINS CAN DIVE DOWN 1,850 FEET (564 M)— DEEPER THAN ANY OTHER BIRD!

Emperor penguins are covered in layers of feathers that act like an insulating blanket. The feathers are so tightly packed that it takes winds of more than 68 miles an hour (110 km/h) to blow them out of place. During winter, the penguins don't move around much, instead staying huddled together in groups to conserve heat and to shelter from the winds. The birds take turns moving to the huddle's toasty interior so they can all stay warm.

Emperor penguins spend nearly the entire long Antarctic winter exposed on the ice—and even hatch their chicks during this season! Female emperors lay a single egg and then immediately leave it behind, heading out to the open ocean to feed on fish, squid, and krill. Females may need to travel 50 miles (80 km) to reach the sea. Meanwhile, male emperor penguins carefully balance the egg on their feet to keep it off the ice and cover it with a feather-fringed pouch of skin to keep it warm. For two months, the males eat nothing. They must stand strong as they are buffeted by snow and wind. When the females finally return, they regurgitate, or bring up, food from their bellies to feed the now hatched chicks. Their duty done, the fathers leave for their own hunting trips. Raising young in the Antarctic isn't easy—but the penguins are experts at teamwork!

THE DEAL WITH SEALS

They lounge on the beach and paddle in the water as if they're enjoying a tropical vacation. But these seals make their home on the seas and shores of Earth's most frigid oceans!

Harp Seals

Almost never making an appearance on land, harp seals prefer to swim in the chilly waters of the North Atlantic and Arctic Oceans. But harp seal pups are born right on the ice, with snowy white coats that help camouflage them against the background and hide them from predators.

Weddell Seals

Weddell seals spend much of their time swimming under the ice of their Antarctic home, emerging through their breathing holes in the spring to rest or give birth. That helps them avoid predators, such as orcas, which almost never venture under the ice for fear of becoming trapped with no way to breathe.

Southern Elephant Seals

The largest of all seals, male southern elephant seals can be more than 20 feet (6 m) long and weigh up to 8,800 pounds (4,000 kg)—about as much as an RV. But their name doesn't come from their massive size: Instead, they're called elephant seals after their trunklike snouts, which they can inflate to make their snorts, grunts, and bellows carry for miles.

THE **RINGED SEAL** GETS ITS NAME FROM THE CIRCULAR PATTERNS ON ITS COAT.

Ringed Seals

These are the most common seals in the Arctic, thriving on the cod and crustaceans that inhabit the cold waters of the Northern Hemisphere. They can dive down 300 feet (91 m) and remain underwater for up to 45 minutes. They use their long claws in their front flippers to dig holes in the ice where they can come up for air. Before surfacing, the seals often blow bubbles upward through the breathing hole to clear away bits of ice and snow so they can see if a polar bear—their main predator—is waiting there to ambush them.

WALRUSES

Enormous at up to 1.5 tons (1.4 t), walruses can be most often found near the Arctic Circle, resting on the ice in groups of hundreds. Though they are related to seals, walruses form their own unique family. Walruses are recognizable by their long tusks, which they use to break breathing holes through the ice from below and to help haul out their massive bodies from the sea. They're also known for their whiskers, which aren't just a fashion statement—they are sensitive detection devices that can sense tiny vibrations in the water, helping the walrus find shellfish in the dark ocean.

ALONG WITH SEALS AND SEA LIONS, WALRUSES BELONG TO A GROUP OF MARINE MAMMALS CALLED PINNIPEDS. THE NAME REFERS TO THEIR FLIPPERED FEET, FROM THE LATIN WORDS *PINNA* ("FIN") AND *PES* ("FOOT").

Ocean Hunters

The ocean holds many skillful hunters, but of them all, orcas are perhaps the ocean's greatest predator. They hunt in groups called pods, using communication and cooperation to take down marine mammals such as sea lions, sharks, and even other whales. Because of this hunting strategy, experts often liken them to wolves.

Orcas can weigh up to 11 tons (10 t) and have bold black-and-white coloring, which helps obscure their outline in the water, confusing prey. Their ability to swim at 30 miles an hour (48 km/h)—faster than many sharks—and their mouths full of three-inch (8-cm)-long, interlocking teeth are fearsome. But it's the orca's smarts that make it a truly deadly hunter.

Orcas are the largest members of the dolphin family. Like dolphins, they have large brains and are highly social animals that live in tight-knit pods of about 40 individuals. Each pod of orcas has its own distinct calls that members of the pod can recognize even from a distance. Like wolf packs, pods of orcas roam the sea, working together to capture their next meal.

Different pods develop their own hunting strategies. Some pods charge floating ice in a tight group, creating a huge wave that sweeps any resting seals off the ice and into the water. Other pods will use their tails to stun sharks by smacking them on their heads, then flipping them upside down. Orcas pass down their elders' hunting knowledge to the pod's younger individuals.

THE DORSAL FIN OF A **MALE ORCA** CAN GROW TO BE SIX FEET (1.8 M) TALL.

Unicorns of the Sea

For centuries, adventurers who journeyed to the northernmost part of the world came back bearing long, spiraled horns. They sold these horns at ancient European marketplaces, claiming they had belonged to unicorns, and monarchs paid hefty sums to own one. Kings and queens wielded scepters and drank from cups made from the horns, and it's rumored that England's Queen Elizabeth I paid 10,000 pounds—the price of a castle at the time—to own one.

These horns didn't belong to unicorns. They came from narwhals, a species of whale that lives in the icy waters of the Arctic.

A narwhal's tusk (grown usually—but not always—by males) is actually a tooth that grows right through the animal's upper lip, reaching lengths of up to 10 feet (3 m). The tusk is packed with nerves and dotted with tiny holes that allow seawater to enter. Some scientists think narwhals may use their unusual protrusion to sense underwater sounds or battle other narwhals in competitions for mates. Because narwhals are skittish and live in the cold, isolated Arctic, it's difficult for experts to see them in action and find out for sure.

But they're getting closer: In 2017, researchers saw narwhals using their tusks in person. Two camera drones in a northeastern region of Canada called Tremblay Sound, Nunavut, captured footage of narwhals wielding their tusks to hit arctic cod, stunning the fish and temporarily immobilizing them so the narwhals could gulp them down. The mystery of the elongated appendage may be partly solved—but there is plenty left to learn about these secretive tusked whales of the north.

NARWHALS CHANGE COLOR AS THEY AGE, TURNING FROM BLUE-GRAY AS NEWBORNS, TO MOTTLED GRAY AS ADULTS, TO NEARLY ALL WHITE IN OLD AGE.

CHILLY SWIMMERS

Polar oceans are so cold that they can drop below 32°F (0°C), the point at which freshwater freezes. At these extreme temperatures, most fish could not survive. But some polar fish have developed incredible adaptations that allow them to thrive in the cold.

Black Rockcod

When temperatures drop on land, animals like some bears and bats hibernate to wait out the cold winter. But fish don't hibernate—at least, scientists didn't think so until 2008. That's when they discovered a species of antarctic cod that goes dormant during the lightless Antarctic winter, becoming 20 times less active. That helps it save its energy during the winter season when food is scarce.

Icefish

Most creatures on Earth have blood that is red in color because of a molecule called hemoglobin, which carries oxygen. But icefish have no hemoglobin—which makes their blood clear! This clear blood is also unusually thin, so the fish can circulate using less energy.

Antarctic Toothfish

While most cold-water fish are small in size, antarctic toothfish can grow longer than 6.5 feet (2 m) and weigh more than 330 pounds (150 kg). They survive by producing anti-freeze proteins in their blood that keep them from freezing, like many other polar fish.

Antarctic Krill

Krill are so hardy that they can go 200 days without eating, even using their own body proteins as a source of energy. There are more than 551 million tons (500 million t) of krill in the Antarctic waters, such a vast number that they often make the sea appear reddish brown in color.

Arctic Cod

Cold Arctic waters would cause the blood of most creatures to freeze solid, swiftly killing them. But the blood of arctic cod contains a special protein that acts like anti-freeze, keeping the blood liquid even when temperatures drop. It works by binding to ice crystals and stopping them from growing larger.

SEA SLEUTHS

IT'S IMPOSSIBLE TO FARM IN THE TUNDRA, SO THE **INUIT** TRADITIONALLY SURVIVED BY HUNTING.

Arctic Experts

Nobody knows more about the Arctic and its animals than the people who live there. In parts of the polar north, the Inuit and other indigenous people hunt polar bears, just as their ancestors have for generations—a task that requires detailed knowledge about their environment. (Today, regulations ensure they don't take enough bears to harm the population.) Hunting polar bears is an essential part of their traditional diet, income, and culture. And it also gives these native communities a front-row seat to the impacts of a changing climate.

That's why a team of researchers led by Kristin Laidre, a marine biologist at the University of Washington in Seattle, Washington, U.S.A., decided to get their perspective. Between December 2014 and March 2015, the team interviewed hunters in two communities, called Tasiilaq and Ittoqqortoormiit, along Greenland's eastern coasts. They asked questions about the bears' habitat, health, and behavior.

The hunters painted a picture of a swiftly changing environment. They described sea ice that's freezing later and melting earlier than it ever has before. While they used to hunt by dogsled, weak and thinning ice has made that so dangerous that many now use only boats. They reported that hungry polar bears were coming into their villages in search of food. And hunters reported finding things polar bears don't usually eat inside the stomachs of dead bears, including dog food, bird eggs, and seaweed.

In a place such as the Arctic—so cold and remote that it's difficult for researchers to work there—these observations by indigenous people provide valuable scientific information. In Alaska, data gathered by locals has already helped scientists discover previously unknown details about the area's bowhead whales. Now, new information about polar bears could help scientists better understand the impact of climate change, and perhaps come up with new ways to help polar bears survive in their shifting world.

Deep Down

Squeeze inside a submersible and sink beneath the ocean's waves. Keep descending, down past the sunlit surface water, down past teeming schools of fish, down past frolicking pods of dolphins and solitary sharks on the hunt. Go deeper still, to where the light fades to blackness and the pressure is so intense that you'd be crushed without the protection of your underwater vehicle. You have reached the deep sea. It is a world without sunlight that is unimaginably cold. In this dark void, it is impossible to judge distances or even tell up from down. And the creatures that live here are unlike anything else on land or sea.

Adventures Down Below

Adventure's waiting down below
in places only you can go.
Deep beyond the sun's bright light
where twilight turns to deepest night,
you'll try your might and test your stuff
(that is, if you are brave enough).
Dive deeper down, explorers bold,
into the blackened waters cold.
Yes—stay the watery course to see
a wondrous deep-sea galaxy.
Sight goblin sharks and dragonfish,
use magic vents to make a wish.
Do battle with a giant squid!
(Or if you don't, just say you did.)
See bioluminescent worlds
of glowing gulpers, jellies pearled,
the swirling scenes of lime-green eyes
and stars in arms of octopi.
And when you've had enough, set sail;
come back above to tell your tale.

—Paige Towler

A GROUP OF JELLIES IS CALLED A **SMACK.**

Go With the Glow

Take a swim in Norway's Trondheim Fjord and there might be something unusual lurking in the water beneath you: thousands upon thousands of delicate pink helmet jellies, which come here to swim in vast numbers.

Helmet jellies, named for the distinctive shape of their bodies, or bells, are found in every ocean of the world except the Arctic. Most of the time, they live far beneath the surface of the sea, 3,000 feet (914 m) down. The largest specimens are found in the Antarctic region, where they can reach 10 inches (25 cm) across and 14 inches (35 cm) long. They can also live for 30 years—an impressively long life given that most jellies live for only months!

During the day, helmet jellies hide in the safety of the deep ocean. Like most types of creatures that live at this lightless depth, they are bioluminescent—meaning they have the ability to produce their own light. How brightly do they glow? Scientists have conducted lab experiments in which they've put a single helmet jelly in a bucket and turned the lights off. They then knocked on the container, causing the jelly to produce enough light that the researchers could see each other in the darkened room.

It's only one of this creature's curious traits. Even though helmet jellies and other species sometimes come together in large groups, they are not considered social animals. But in recent years, scientists have observed them seeming to team up in groups of two or three during the day, when the animals rise to the water's surface to hunt. Individual jellies seem to change their swimming patterns to sync up with their neighbors. Perhaps, scientists think, they are working together to chase down a meal. But how they do so is a mystery: Jellies don't have true eyes and only the simplest of other sensory organs. How do they find each other in the blackness of the deep ocean ... and why?

WHAT'S GLOWING ON?

Only the faintest glimmer of light penetrates the upper regions of the deep sea. Lower still, there is no light at all. Yet people who dive to the deepest regions of the ocean are greeted with a spectacular show. Flashes of blue and green light float, swirl, and zoom through the blackness. This light doesn't come from the sun—it's created by the animals that make this dark place home.

The glow, called bioluminescence, is produced by a chemical reaction that then produces light. To create this reaction, an organism must have special substances in its body called luciferins. Some creatures produce luciferin in their own bodies, while others act as a host to bacteria that carry it.

On land, bioluminescence is rare. Only a few organisms, such as fireflies and glowworms, have the ability. But in the deep sea, it's extremely common. More than 90 percent of all animals in the deep ocean are bioluminescent! Scientists think they use their glowing ability for many different purposes.

Some creatures use bioluminescence to find or attract prey. Certain lanternfish have glowing spots on their heads that light up what's in front of them like a headlamp. That helps them locate prey in the darkness of the deep sea. Others use bioluminescence as a defense. When attacked, a brittle star will shed a glowing limb that flashes to distract the predator as the animal makes a sneaky escape.

Most bioluminescence is bluish in color. That's because blue travels farthest in water. Because red light does not travel far in water, many deep-sea animals cannot see red light at all. A few animals have evolved the ability to take advantage of this: The dragonfish, for example, can both see and produce red light. It shines a spotlight of red light when hunting, using it to seek out prey without them having any idea that they are being watched. Sneaky!

HAWAIIAN BOBTAIL SQUID

EXPERTS THINK
BIOLUMINESCENCE
MAY BE THE MOST
COMMON FORM OF
COMMUNICATION
ON THE PLANET.

THE TWILIGHT ZONE

Between 650 and 3,300 feet (200 and 1,000 m) below the surface, the light of the sun is so weak that it's invisible to the human eye. The water is perpetually cold, around 40°F (4°C). This realm is known as the twilight zone. And the creatures that live here are strange indeed.

Hatchetfish

This fish—named for the hatchetlike shape of its body, sports rows of light-producing organs along its belly. But unlike other fish, hatchetfish don't use the light for hunting. Instead, they regulate the glow—which is blue in color—to match the exact shade of the light filtering down from above. This is called counterillumination, and it makes them nearly invisible to predators looking up from below.

Glass Squid

Most squid squirt ink to distract predators. But that technique doesn't work so well in the darkness of the twilight zone. So instead, some species of glass squid pull their vulnerable tentacles and head inside their body cavity, then fill it with ink, turning themselves into a nasty-tasting ball.

Sloane's Viperfish

The Sloane's viperfish has some of the biggest teeth for its body size in the animal kingdom. They're so oversize they don't fully fit inside the fish's mouth! Instead of biting prey, Sloane's viperfish use their teeth like a cage, closing them to trap the creatures inside. Then—gulp!

Lanternfish

These big-eyed fish—the better to see with in the dimness of the twilight zone—are named for their ability to produce light. Tiny organs along the fish's underside produce a glow that attracts other small fish. When they come in close to investigate, they become the lanternfish's dinner.

Firefly Squid

Firefly squid spend most of their lives far out of sight in the deep ocean. But each year from March to June, they flock to Toyama Bay, Japan, where they come to release their eggs. Each one emits electric blue light from its tentacles, and when millions come together on shore, they create a dazzling display.

THE MIDNIGHT ZONE

The region of the sea below 3,300 feet (1,000 m) is the most unexplored place on the entire planet. It's called the midnight zone. Here, there is complete darkness, and intense pressure 400 times greater than that at the surface. It's an extreme environment—and it's home to extreme animals.

Telescope Octopuses

Very little is known about this rare octopus that spends its days floating through Earth's deepest oceans. It's named for its odd eyes that protrude from its body on stalks, which it can rotate—probably to help it spot predators or prey swimming off to the side.

Deep-Sea Dragonfish

This eel-like fish sports a strange facial accessory: a glowing barbel, or whisker-like protrusion, from its lower jaw. Fish swim in close to the glowing barbel, thinking it's food—but then they become the dragonfish's food instead. It is a fish with its own fishing lure!

Vampire Squid

It's named for its dark color and the skin that connects its arms, which resembles a vampire's cape. But the vampire squid is not a frightening bloodsucker: It eats by using its sticky tentacles to capture detritus, tiny particles of food that float down from the sea surface. When scared, the vampire squid can pull its cloak up over its body—like an umbrella flipped inside out—to expose its spine-covered underside.

Giant Oarfish

Oarfish, the longest species of bony fish ever discovered, can reach 56 feet (17 m) long and weigh up to 600 pounds (270 kg). Experts think that this long, slender fish could have been the inspiration for ancient tales of sea serpents.

Gulper Eels

Most of the time, this strange creature swims along like a regular eel, eating small crustaceans. But when it feels threatened—or when it encounters prey too large to eat easily, the gulper eel can inflate its huge mouth to enormous proportions. Now that's what you call a big gulp!

Call It an Aww-ctopus

As far as 13,100 feet (4,000 m) down—and perhaps much deeper—lives the deepest-dwelling octopus in the sea. Some would say the Dumbo octopus, named for the pair of fins that make it resemble the cartoon elephant, is also the most adorable octopus there is.

There isn't only one type of Dumbo octopus; more than a dozen species belong to a group called umbrella octopuses for the web of skin they sport between their arms. All Dumbo octopuses have earlike fins, which they flap to help them move through the water. They can also contract their webbed arms (like closing an umbrella) to get a burst of speed if they need to evade a predator, such as a shark.

Most Dumbo octopuses are small—at 10 inches (25 cm), only a bit larger than a guinea pig—though some can be six feet (1.8 m) in length. Like their relatives that live in shallower waters, Dumbo octopuses can change their color at will. But, unlike most other octopuses, the Dumbo octopus cannot squirt ink—it wouldn't do them much good in the darkness of the deep sea! Instead, some have arms lined with sharp spines that they use for defense.

Dumbo octopuses are rarely spotted, and their environment is hard to reach. That means scientists are only beginning to learn about these adorable denizens of the deep.

DUMBO OCTOPUSES SLURP UP THEIR PREY WHOLE.

Chambered Nautiluses

The Living Fossil

Before fish first appeared, it was the chambered nautilus that ruled Earth's oceans. This cousin of the octopus and squid has hardly changed for hundreds of millions of years, offering a glimpse of what life was like in prehistoric seas. There were once about 10,000 species of these animals, but only a handful of species survive today.

Nautiluses have simple eyes that can sense only light and dark, but that doesn't slow them down. To explore their world, they use their sense of smell and their 90 tentacles—the most of any creature in the cephalopod family. The tentacles are covered with grooves and ridges, which help the nautilus grip food and pull it in to its parrotlike beak.

The nautilus's shell never stops growing. Unlike a snail's, it's divided into chambers.

As the animal gets bigger (adults can be eight inches [20 cm] long), it moves into the newest, largest one. The inner chambers are filled with gas. Much like a submarine, the nautilus pumps liquid in and out of these chambers to dive down or rise up in the water.

During the day, nautiluses avoid predators by hiding in the deep sea. Then, at night, they migrate to shallower waters to hunt among the coral reefs. To move, these animals use a system of jet propulsion, squirting water through a tube called a siphon to shoot themselves along backward.

MOST
ANGLERFISH
ARE SMALL, BUT
SOME CAN REACH
3.3 FEET (1 M) IN
LENGTH.

ANGLERFISH
WERE "FISHING"
LONG BEFORE HUMAN
ANGLERS: THEY FIRST
APPEARED IN EARTH'S
OCEANS AS LONG AS
130 MILLION
YEARS AGO!

Deep Sea Anglerfish

LURED IN

The deep sea is full of strange-looking creatures with transparent bodies, gnashing jaws, and glow-in-the-dark limbs. But the deep sea anglerfish may be the most bizarre of them all.

There are more than 200 species of anglerfish, and nearly all of them live in the cold, dark depths of the Atlantic Ocean and waters around the Antarctic, as deep as a mile (1.6 km) below the surface. Their enormous, gaping mouths give them a permanently angry expression. Their skin is specially adapted to reflect blue light—the color of light emitted by nearly all bioluminescent creatures. That makes the anglerfish nearly invisible to other animals.

The anglerfish's strangest feature is the spike that protrudes from the snout of the female angler. It looks like a fishing pole—giving the anglerfish its name—and the fish uses it like one, too. It's tipped with an orb that glows with light, thanks to millions of bioluminescent bacteria that live inside. The anglerfish's basketball-shaped body means it's not an agile swimmer—but it doesn't have to be. Anglerfish hunt by remaining motionless, the glowing lure at the end of their "fishing pole" swaying back and forth to attract prey. When an unsuspecting fish swims close enough, the anglerfish snaps it up with its powerful jaws and swallows it whole. Both the anglerfish's jaws and stomach expand to massive proportions, allowing it to gulp down prey twice the size of its body.

It's hard to find a mate in the vast darkness of the deep sea. So male anglerfish employ an extremely unusual strategy to find females: When a young anglerfish male, which is much smaller than the female, comes across a potential mate, he grabs onto her side with his sharp teeth and holds tight. Over time, his internal organs melt away and his body fuses to hers, transforming him into a parasite that feeds off of her body. More than six males can attach themselves to a single female.

DEEP-SEA SHARKS

They have snapping jaws and sharp teeth. But otherwise, these sharks look very different from their cousins closer to the surface. Each one has unique traits that help it survive in the harsh conditions of the deep sea.

Goblin Sharks

As the goblin shark closes in on its prey, a squid, the smaller creature darts just out of reach—or so it thinks. The shark shoots its jaw three inches (8 cm) out of its mouth, snapping up the squid! After eating, the shark slides its jaw back and swims off for its next victim.

Greenland Sharks

Scarce food and super-cold temperatures mean that many animals of the deep sea grow slowly—and that some can live an incredibly long time, too. Scientists think that some Greenland sharks, the largest fish in the Arctic at 24 feet (7.3 m), could be as much as 400 years old.

Cookiecutter Sharks

This little shark, about 20 inches (51 cm) in length, has a ferocious feeding strategy: It uses its lips to suction itself to the side of a much larger victim, such as a bluefin tuna or a great white shark. Then it uses its sharp teeth to scoop out a mouth-size bite, leaving behind a wound that resembles the work of a cookie cutter.

Bluntnose Sixgill Sharks

Scientists believe this animal is descended from sharks that roamed Earth's oceans even before dinosaurs walked the land. Named for the extra gills they have compared with most sharks' five, bluntnose sixgills are true deep-sea dwellers, spending most of their time 4,500 feet (1,372 m) below the surface.

Frilled Sharks

These odd sharks have a snakelike body, rows of three-pronged teeth, and the frilly-looking gill slits that give them their name. Frilled sharks are sometimes called living fossils because they have changed little in 80 million years. Not much is known about them—except that their strange-shaped teeth are perfect for hooking their preferred prey: soft-bodied squid.

SEA SLEUTHS

SCIENTISTS BELIEVE THE FIRST LIVING THINGS ON OUR PLANET MAY HAVE ORIGINATED NEAR VOLCANOES IN OCEAN TRENCHES.

JACQUES PICCARD AND DON WALSH WAVE FROM THEIR SUBMERSIBLE, THE *TRIESTE*, AFTER THEIR DESCENT TO THE CHALLENGER DEEP.

The Voyage to the Bottom

Twelve people in history have walked on the moon. If that seems like a small number, consider this: Only four people have been to the deepest point on our own planet, located in the Mariana Trench.

The Mariana Trench is in the western Pacific Ocean, a valley in the seafloor that runs for about 1,500 miles (2,400 km) and extends down nearly seven miles (11 km). That's so deep that if the world's tallest mountain—Mount Everest—was dropped inside, the top of its peak would still be more than a mile (1.6 km) underwater! At the bottom of the Mariana Trench, conditions are perpetually dark, temperatures are only a few degrees above freezing, and the water pressure is an unimaginably crushing eight tons per square inch (1.1 t/sq cm), or about a thousand times the pressure at sea level. It's no wonder it went entirely unexplored until 1960.

It was January 23 of that year that U.S. Navy Lt. Don Walsh and Swiss engineer Jacques Piccard boarded an experimental submersible called the *Trieste* and began the long trip to the bottom of the sea. At 31,000 feet (9,400 m) below sea level, they heard a loud crack. They checked their instruments, found no signs of immediate danger, and kept going. After nearly five hours inside a tiny cabin only six feet four inches (1.9 m) across, they touched down at the deepest point on Earth. (The alarming sound turned out to be caused by a cracking window near the submarine's entrance tunnel, safely separated from the crew cabin by a steel hatch.)

On their way down, Walsh and Piccard saw floating dots of light through the porthole—swarms of bioluminescent creatures. On the seabed, they saw a creature that Piccard described as "some type of flatfish," revealing for the first time that life could indeed survive at such an extreme depth. It was a historic discovery that forever changed our understanding of the planet. Yet only two other people—the filmmaker James Cameron, in 2012, and explorer Victor Vescovo, in 2019—have ever made the dangerous journey. Today, scientists use unmanned robots to explore the ocean's trenches. But much about this dark, desolate world has yet to be discovered.

Extreme Ocean

The depths of the ocean are the least-known region of our planet. It's no wonder: To explore them, scientists must climb into one of the handful of submersibles on the planet capable of diving to the bottom of the sea, or send remotely operated vehicles in their place. But the ocean's most hidden realms are keeping some of our planet's most astounding secrets: massive underwater mountains, geysers that spew superheated noxious water, and all kinds of living things that make these alien places their home.

The Myth of the Kraken

It's the most fearsome sea monster that's ever been imagined. The ancient Norse said it haunted the seas, lurking unseen beneath the surface of the water. Fishermen, it was said, would suddenly find themselves surrounded by schools of fish, practically leaping into their nets. They would rejoice at their luck ... until they realized that something was scaring the fish toward the surface: the Kraken.

Centuries of folktales spun the story even scarier. The Kraken was said to be the length of 10 ships, or so big its body, bobbing upon the surface, looked like an island that hapless sailors tried to land on. Respected scientists listed the Kraken as a real creature. Even as recently as the mid-1800s, sailors continued to argue that they really did sometimes encounter a sea creature of monstrous size.

They were right. In 1853, an enormous creature washed up from the deep sea and became stranded on a Danish beach. It was one of humankind's first sightings of the real-life animal that most likely inspired the legendary Kraken: the giant squid.

These deep-sea dwellers are true giants: The largest individual ever recorded was nearly 43 feet (13 m) long (including tentacles), with eyes the size of soccer balls. Because they make their home in the vast deep sea, these huge animals are almost never spotted. Much about them is a mystery, though scientists have learned something from the giant squid beaks they've found in the stomachs of decaying sperm whales—and the large circular scars, made by enormous suckers, that mark the whales' skin. These are clues that these two colossal creatures duke it out in epic battles at the bottom of the sea.

SQUID HAVE THREE HEARTS AND BLUE BLOOD.

UNDERSEA MOUNTAINS

Atop the island of Hawaii sits Mauna Kea, a dormant volcano that towers 13,796 feet (4,205 m) above sea level. But most of the mountain's bulk is actually hiding underwater: Mauna Kea is only the very tip of an enormous undersea mountain, or seamount. Measured from its base on the seafloor, Mauna Kea is 32,696 feet (9,966 m) tall—taller than Mount Everest!

Seamounts are most often found near the edges of tectonic plates, the enormous pieces of Earth's crust that fit together like a jigsaw puzzle. These plates bump and jostle against each other with the movement of the flow of molten rock beneath. In some areas, plates collide, forcing parts of the Earth's crust down, where it melts in our planet's hot interior, rises back to the surface, and erupts. This process creates seamounts. Many seamounts were formed millions of years ago, but some are active volcanoes in the process of being born. Scientists are only beginning to dive into the world of seamounts: There are estimated to be about 30,000 seamounts in the world, and only a handful have been explored.

Seamounts give ocean organisms something to cling to, and currents swirl around their slopes, carrying nutrients for a wide variety of marine creatures. Many of them live nowhere else in the world than on their particular underwater mountain.

SEAMOUNTS ARE FOUND IN **EVERY OCEAN** ON EARTH.

MAUNA KEA

Scalloped Hammerhead Sharks

These sharks can often be seen gathering by the hundreds near sea-mounts. In an undersea dance, they circle the underwater mountains, females on the inside and males on the outer edge. One expert wonders whether the sharks use seamounts as gathering places and if the magnetic fields of the lava flows there could act as a compass to guide them as they go.

Sea Lillies

Looking more like a plant than an animal, sea lilies have long stalks that attach them to the ocean floor and feathery arms that wave gently with the movement of the water. For a long time, scientists thought they were stuck in place like plants. But in the 1980s, they were astounded to see sea lilies shed their stalk ends to free themselves from the seafloor and crawl around with their arms.

Deep-Water Corals

When we picture coral reefs, we think of warm, tropical waters. But corals can also live deep in the ocean, in waters as cold as 39°F (4°C). Unlike tropical corals, deep-water corals don't need sunlight to survive, because they don't have photosynthetic algae living inside them. Instead, these corals fend for themselves by capturing edible particles from the water.

LIFE AT THE LIMITS

Until not so very long ago, experts thought that the bottom of the sea was a barren desert, inhospitable to life. Then, in 1977, scientists dragging a camera device along the ocean floor from a boat near the Galápagos Islands recorded something strange: an unusual spike in temperature. When they reviewed the photos their camera had taken at that spot, they were shocked: There were crowds of clams and mussels at the bottom of the sea. Two days later, a team of scientists plunged 8,000 feet (2,400 m) to the ocean floor in a research submersible to investigate. They were stunned by what they found there: Surprisingly warm water, reaching 46°F (7.8°C), was bubbling with minerals toxic to most animals—and it was absolutely teeming with living things, most of them unknown to science.

The researchers had discovered a hydrothermal vent, a type of deep-sea geyser on the ocean floor that forms along mid-ocean ridges, where tectonic plates spread apart, allowing superheated magma to rise up from the depths of the planet. The magma heats seawater and dissolves into it all kinds of chemicals, such as sulfur and calcium. This enriched water can reach nearly 750°F (400°C).

Unlike all other life on Earth, the creatures that make their home on hydrothermal vents do not depend on the sun to survive. Instead, bacteria there use the chemicals spewing from deep within Earth as a source for energy, a process called chemosynthesis. Other hydro-thermal vent organisms in turn depend on the bacteria for food. This finding was hailed as one of the greatest discoveries of the 20th century, and it changed our understanding of how life can arise.

Giant Tube Worms

These strange worms, topped with bright red plumes, are giant in size, some growing up to eight feet (2.4 m) in length. They have no mouth and no digestive tract. Instead of eating, they depend on the bacteria that live inside them for food. The bacteria convert chemicals from the hydrothermal vents into molecules the worms need to survive.

Zoarcid Fish

Also called the eelpout fish, this two-foot (0.6-m)-long swimmer spends its days floating nearly motionless around clumps of giant tube worms. Despite their relaxed lifestyle, they are top predators in vent communities, feasting on everything from tube worms to shrimps to crabs.

Yeti Crabs

This crab's hairy arms led scientists to name it after the mythical abominable snowman. Since their discovery in 2005, the crabs have been spotted holding their claws over plumes of hot water coming out of hydrothermal vents. Scientists think they are likely "farming" bacteria that cling to their hairs so they can eat it, waving their claws through the water to provide the bacteria with a flow of nutrients.

SECOND LIFE

When a ship sinks below the surface, it might seem that it is no longer useful. But as it settles on the seafloor, the ship's second life—as a home for sea creatures—is only beginning. On the endless sandy seafloor of the deep ocean, the hard surfaces and nooks and crannies of a shipwreck are a haven for all kinds of creatures. Anemones and mussels grip to what were once decks and cabins. These in turn attract bigger critters such as sea stars, crabs, and fish.

In 2011, scientists wiggled into scuba suits and dived into the waters off the coast of North Carolina, U.S.A. The area is known as the Graveyard of the Atlantic because it holds dozens of ships that sank when they were struck during World War II. When diving scientists arrived at the wrecks—nearly 70 years since they came to rest on the ocean floor—they found that the ghostly vessels had been transformed into thriving marine ecosystems. At four shipwreck sites, scientists found about 40 species.

In warm waters, shipwrecks can act as artificial reefs. Tiny coral polyps land on their surfaces, take hold, and build their hard skeletons. Over time, the ship becomes totally encrusted in colorful coral, which provides a home for a diverse population of tropical plants and animals. As coral reefs are disappearing from the oceans at an alarming rate (see p. 59), shipwrecks may provide a new hope for these creatures.

IN THE 1800S, SOME PEOPLE THREW LOGS INTO RIVERS TO CREATE **HABITATS** FOR FISH THEY COULD LATER CATCH.

SHIPWRECK SPECIES

Lost at sea? Not these creatures. They make their lives on the wrecks of ships that no longer sail the seven seas.

DOLPHINFISH
Also known as mahi-mahi, this ocean predator can reach 6.5 feet (2 m). Dolphinfish are strong swimmers that are known for their ability to capture squid, sharks, and even flying fish, their favorite prey.

FAN WORMS
Like flowers of the sea, fan worms spread their brightly colored tentacles into the water, searching for tiny specks of food. If a fish gets too close, the creature will pull its spray of tentacles backward into its tube-shaped body to keep safe.

GRAY TRIGGERFISH
When threatened, these fish can squeeze into a crevice on the wreck and wedge themselves into place by sticking up a front spine. In that protected position, the fish are tough for a predator to pull out.

SEA SLEUTHS

TOPOGRAPHY IS THE ARRANGEMENT OF AN AREA'S PHYSICAL FEATURES, SUCH AS VALLEYS AND MOUNTAINS.

BECAUSE NAVY RULES MEANT THARP COULDN'T BOARD **RESEARCH VESSELS** LIKE HER MALE COLLEAGUES, SHE DID ALL HER EARLY WORK WITHOUT EVER SETTING FOOT ON A SHIP.

Mapping the Ocean Floor

The bottom of the ocean is so unexplored that scientists know more about the topography of the moon and Mars than they do about the topography of the seafloor. But if it weren't for the discoveries of a little-known scientist named Marie Tharp, we would know a lot less.

Born in 1920 in Ypsilanti, Michigan, U.S.A., Tharp grew up during a time when women were not welcome in the sciences. But she was thirsty for knowledge. When most young men were overseas fighting World War II, the vacancies opened up an opportunity for female students in the geology department at the University of Michigan, and Tharp seized it. After earning degrees first in geology and then in mathematics, Tharp landed a position in the Lamont Geological Laboratory at Columbia University in New York City.

There, it was her task as a research assistant to analyze sonar readings taken by ships criss-crossing the ocean. Sonar, a technology that had become advanced during the war, uses sound to "see" into the water by emitting pings and then listening for the echoes as they bounce off the ocean floor. As she meticulously plotted the data, Tharp peered for the first time into a secret world. What scientists had thought was a flat, muddy plain forming the bottom of the sea was actually a surface as varied as the land, with canyons and mountain ranges.

As Tharp continued to draw her findings, creating the world's first maps of the ocean floor, she was struck by an astounding discovery: a deep trench splitting a mountain range that ran along the entire Atlantic Ocean. Tharp thought it must be a rift valley, an area where Earth's crust is split, and magma is rising up from deep inside it. But while some scientists thought that Earth's surface consists of separate plates that gradually shift position, the idea was controversial at the time. More data eventually confirmed that Tharp was right. Today, the concept of the movement of Earth's plates makes up the foundation of the field of geology. Tharp changed science forever, and along the way, revealed the most hidden reaches of our planet.

People and Oceans

The oceans are home to a truly incredible array of life. Whether you're diving to the deepest seafloor in a submersible or simply dipping your toes in the waves at the coast, you're sure to encounter a range of remarkable creatures. There are scuttling crabs, leaping dolphins, majestic whales, colorful reef creatures, bioluminescent fish, and much more. People have spent thousands of years exploring the ocean's waters and discovering its life. But the ocean isn't only there for us to admire. We depend on it for food, jobs, and more than half of the very oxygen we breathe. Now humans are putting the ocean in danger—but we also have the ability to protect it.

INTO THE UNKNOWN

For as long as there have been humans, we have gazed at the ocean and wondered what secrets its waters were hiding. Beginning thousands of years ago, people started exploring the ocean, first traveling across its surface to new lands and later diving beneath the waves to discover the undersea world.

Peoples living in present-day Australia, Indonesia, and other Southeast Asian islands are the first to cross the sea. With no tools of modern navigation, they observe ocean currents and use the positions of the stars to find their way across thousands of miles of open ocean.

4000 B.C.

The Greeks invent a device called a diving bell—an air-filled chamber that people can enter to explore under-water. They first use it to clear debris from harbors to keep ships safe during wartime.

360 B.C.

A Dutch inventor named Cornelis Drebbel invents the world's first submarine and uses it to dive 15 feet (4.6 m) below the surface of England's River Thames. Since no plans survive, historians can only guess how it worked.

ca 1620

Geologist and cartographer Marie Tharp discovers the Mid-Atlantic Ridge, changing geology forever (see p. 168).

1953

Don Walsh and Jacques Piccard dive to the deepest part of the ocean—a portion of the Mariana Trench called Challenger Deep—and observe deep-sea life (see p. 156).

1960

Scientists aboard the deep-sea vehicle *Alvin* discover hydrothermal vents and the strange sea life that survives there (see p. 164).

1977

Modern oceanography begins with the Challenger expedition, the first seafaring mission organized to gather data on ocean features such as temperature, currents, and marine life. One of its many discoveries is the deepest part of the ocean, a trench in the Pacific now known as the Mariana Trench.

Two scientists named William Beebe and Otis Barton cram into a tiny steel sphere that's only four feet nine inches (1.4 m) across and plunge beneath the ocean waves to explore deeper than anyone had ever been before. They reach a depth of more than 3,000 feet (914 m) off the coast of Bermuda and discover a mysterious world of bioluminescent creatures.

Underwater explorer Jacques Cousteau, along with engineer Émile Gagnan, develops the first modern scuba system, called the Aqua-Lung. This invention revolutionizes oceanography, allowing divers to stay underwater for extended periods of time to explore the world under the sea.

1872

1934

1943

Off the coast of Oahu, Hawaii, American oceanographer and explorer Sylvia Earle descends 1,250 feet (381 m) wearing an armored diving suit and strapped to the front of a submersible. She untethers herself from the research vehicle and explores the seafloor, setting the record for the deepest untethered dive.

The Census of Marine Life, a 10-year project involving more than 2,000 scientists from 80 countries, is completed. The program catalogs the living things in all the world's oceans, greatly expanding scientific knowledge of marine life.

1979

2010

173

WHY THE OCEAN MATTERS

You may live near the coast, or you may have only visited the ocean in books and films. But no matter how far you live from the shore, the ocean plays a big role in your life.

The ocean is the planet's life-support system. With every breath we take, our lungs fill with oxygen that comes from ocean plants. Ocean water helps make our planet livable by soaking up heat from the sun and carrying it around the planet through currents. And it absorbs carbon dioxide from the atmosphere, helping regulate our climate.

Coastal areas provide a home for billions of people. About 44 percent of people live within 93 miles (150 km) of the ocean. Humans have been building settlements near the ocean since the beginning of civilization, and today, the majority of the top 10 largest cities on Earth are located by the coast. From these cities by the sea, we travel across the ocean to explore new places and transport goods. Ships carry around 90 percent of the goods that are traded between countries.

The oceans are also an important source of food. More than one billion people depend on fish as a major part of their diet. Early humans used fishing rods, spears, traps, and handheld nets to fish. This kind of fishing is still practiced in some parts of the world today, but most ocean fish sold is now caught by commercial fishing vessels, which often use huge nets to scoop up fish, damaging the seafloor and harming marine life as they go. Though humans rely on the ocean for survival, we are now causing the oceans great harm, putting the future of our planet and all its living things at risk.

STILT FISHING IS A TRADITIONAL FISHING METHOD IN THE ISLAND NATION OF SRI LANKA.

OCEANS ARE THE PLANET'S LARGEST HABITAT.

OUR CHANGING SEAS

Human activities are impacting the oceans in many ways. One is overfishing. In the mid-20th century, industrial fishing fleets started developing technology for finding and catching massive quantities of fish. Soon, humans were taking more fish than the ocean could replace. Now the populations of certain species, such as Atlantic bluefin tuna, have declined so much that they are in danger of becoming extinct. Scientists estimated that in 2003, there were only 10 percent of the numbers of large ocean fish left compared to what there were before industrial fishing began.

Pollution is also a major threat to the oceans. Plastic trash, sewage from factories, oil from oil spills, and pesticides and fertilizer from farms are all washed into the water supply and out into the ocean. These substances can kill marine plants and animals. They can also cause species such as poisonous algae (see p. 90 about red tides) to grow out of control, harming sea life in those areas.

Climate change is affecting our oceans, too. Scientific data shows that the temperature of the sea surface has increased by as much as 0.2°F (.13°C) per decade between 1971 and 2010. As water warms, it expands. In addition, warmer water melts ice at the poles. Both those factors have caused Earth's sea levels to rise by around nine inches (23 cm) over the past century. And about one-quarter of the carbon dioxide released by burning coal, oil, and gas dissolves into the ocean. That has caused ocean water to become 30 percent more acidic over the past 200 years, an effect called ocean acidification.

All these changes take a toll on ocean life. In response to warming temperatures, coral reefs are suffering (see p. 59 about coral bleaching), and fish are moving to different areas. Some animals, such as polar bears (see p. 132), are losing their homes, while others, such as sea turtles (see pp. 20 and 116), are having trouble reproducing. And because we are still learning about the ocean, we don't fully understand the impact we are making on the world's waters.

PROTECTING MARINE PLACES

Today, about 15 percent of the world's land is protected from development. That includes national parks and forests, where animals and plants are allowed to live undisturbed by humans. Some scientists think that the best way to keep the oceans healthy is to protect undersea regions, too.

Because the oceans are mostly hidden from human view, it took us longer to understand their importance, and their waters went unprotected for a long time. The first marine protected areas in the United States were created in the early 20th century, starting with Pelican Island National Wildlife Refuge in Florida in 1903. Different marine protected areas have different rules, but all help ensure that marine animals are able to reproduce and grow to their adult size without interference from humans. That helps keep the populations of these animals strong in these areas and the surrounding waters, too. Today, there are more than 5,000 marine protected areas around the world. But together, they cover only about 4 percent of the oceans.

One person who thinks we can do more is Enric Sala, a marine ecologist, or scientist who studies the relationships between the ocean and the creatures that live there. After years spent researching all the ways the ocean was in danger, Sala got tired of just standing by. He wanted to take action. So in 2008, he teamed up with National Geographic to launch an ocean protection project called Pristine Seas.

Now, Sala is searching for the most remote corners of the ocean, "pristine" places that have gone almost untouched by humans. Sala and his team travel to these places and conduct detailed research by scuba diving and by using cameras and submersibles. They get a view of the ocean as it was before it was impacted by overfishing, pollution, and global warming. They use what they find to determine if the region is a good candidate to become a marine protected area. So far, Pristine Seas has created more than 20 marine protected areas covering more than 1.9 million square miles (5 million sq km). Sala hopes that the project will help save Earth's last true wilderness: the ocean.

BECAUSE **PROTECTED AREAS** GIVE YOUNG FISH A SAFE PLACE TO GROW INTO ADULTS, THEY CREATE MORE FISH TO HELP SUSTAIN PEOPLE.

NATIONAL GEOGRAPHIC EXPLORER-IN-RESIDENCE ENRIC SALA DOCUMENTS OBSERVATIONS OF DEEP-SEA FAUNA 800 FEET (250 M) BELOW THE SURFACE OF THE SOUTH PACIFIC OCEAN.

SAVING SHARKS
An Interview With Marine Conservationist Jess Cramp

Jess Cramp is a scientist who loves the sea. She swims, she surfs, she scuba dives, and she's on a mission to help protect one of the most misunderstood creatures in the sea: sharks. Cramp works as a marine conservationist, or a person who advocates to help preserve the ocean and its life.

WERE YOU INTERESTED IN THE OCEAN WHEN YOU WERE A KID?

Yes! Even though I grew up in Pennsylvania, U.S.A., in the mountains, I always had a fascination with the ocean. I had a series of books about ocean explorer Jacques Cousteau, and I read them over and over. When I got older, my college didn't offer marine biology, so instead, I studied biology and chemistry. On the side, I learned to surf and scuba dive. All that prepared me for a career as a marine scientist. You don't have to be from the coast to have a career studying the ocean!

HOW DID YOU BECOME INTERESTED IN SHARKS?

I was on a sailboat anchored in the South Pacific when I decided to jump on my surfboard and surf to shore. After I caught a wave and rode out, I put on my scuba mask for the swim back to the ship. When I peeked underwater, I was amazed at what I saw: There were reef sharks all around me! But I wasn't scared. Instead, I had a realization that we have to do more to protect these creatures.

WHAT KINDS OF DANGERS ARE SHARKS FACING?

The biggest threat to sharks is fishing. Many people know that some sharks are fished for their fins, to make a traditional Chinese dish called shark fin soup. But most people don't know that the majority of sharks are actually fished for their meat and other parts. Others are caught accidentally by fishing boats hunting for tuna or other fish. Many species of sharks don't have babies often—once a year or less. That means that it's really hard for sharks to recover from overfishing.

WHAT ARE YOU DOING TO HELP PROTECT SHARKS?

In 2012, I helped create a shark sanctuary in the Cook Islands. Sharks are now protected from fishing in an area that covers about 772,000 square miles (2 million sq km). Boats caught with sharks on board there are fined. Now I'm monitoring sharks in the area to see what kind of impact the sanctuary has. I am tagging oceanic whitetip sharks with satellite trackers so I can watch their movement patterns through the area. Hopefully, the sanctuary gives the sharks a safe place to reproduce and grow, so that more of them can survive to adulthood.

SOME PEOPLE THINK SHARKS ARE SCARY. WHAT DO YOU THINK?

Seeing a shark in the wild is very special: Shark attacks are incredibly rare. Sharks have evolved with the Earth for about 400 million years. They're an essential part of the ocean ecosystem: We need them around for other creatures to thrive. Plus, check out some species such as wobbegong sharks—they're pretty cute!

"YOU DON'T HAVE TO BE FROM THE COAST TO HAVE A CAREER STUDYING THE OCEAN!"

—Jess Cramp

OCEAN OF PLASTIC

Between the Hawaiian Islands and the coast of California, there is a garbage-clogged stretch of water twice the size of the U.S. state of Texas. Called the Great Pacific Garbage Patch, it's the world's largest collection of floating trash.

All together, more than 1.8 trillion pieces of trash float and swirl here—an amount equivalent to 250 pieces for every person on Earth. From abandoned fishing gear to bottles to pieces of plastic the size of pencil erasers to tiny microplastics, the trash soup stretches from the surface to the seafloor. And it's only one of several garbage patches in the ocean.

More than 40 percent of plastic on our planet is used only once before it's thrown away. And every year, nine million tons (8.2 million t) of that plastic makes its way to the ocean. Because plastics are a relatively recent invention—mass produced for consumers in only the past half century—no one is exactly sure how long they take to decompose. Experts estimate it might be something like 20 years for plastic bags, 450 years for bottles, and 600 years for fishing line.

That plastic trash is bad news for marine life. Animals become entangled in it and often accidentally eat it. Experts estimate that more than half of sea turtles have accidentally eaten plastic trash—probably because floating plastic closely resembles their favorite food: jellyfish. Plastic also smothers coral reefs and clogs the bellies of fish, whales, and seabirds.

MORE THAN **FIVE TRILLION** PIECES OF PLASTIC ARE FLOATING IN THE WORLD'S SEAS.

AN ANTI-POLLUTION REVOLUTION

Environmental scientist Kristal Ambrose saw the ocean plastic problem up close when she sailed across the Pacific Ocean in 2012 to study the Western Garbage Patch (part of the Great Pacific Garbage Patch). After collecting plastic forks, bags, bottle caps, and toothbrushes from the sea, Ambrose realized that these were items she, too, used in her daily life.

She resolved to become part of the solution. In 2014, she founded the Bahamas Plastic Movement, an organization based in South Eleuthera, Bahamas. There, local kids work together to gather information on how much plastic is used by locals and how it's affecting ocean life there. Because of their work, government officials announced a plan to ban plastic bags in the Bahamas.

TURNING THE TIDE

When it comes to the future of the ocean and its life, it's easy to feel helpless. But as these success stories show, when people step in to help, they can make a big difference. These five ocean creatures were once in deep danger. Today, they're making a comeback.

Lingcod

These big-mouthed fish were once -a staple food of indigenous people who lived along the U.S. coastline. But beginning in the 1870s, commercial fisheries began hunting the fish by dragging nets along the seafloor in the area. By 1999, this overfishing had reduced the population to 7.5 percent of its former level. Strict laws were enacted to restrict fishing, and ever since, numbers have been on the rise.

Manta Rays

The largest population of giant manta rays in the world lives in the southeast Pacific, off the coast of South America. In 2012, conservationists began pushing for laws that would keep the mantas from being fished. In 2015, the Peruvian government granted that protection, and today, giant manta swim safely off the shores of Peru during their seasonal migration. Conservationists hope that these measures will help mantas survive into the future.

Gray Whales

Gray whales are some of Earth's most impressive long-distance travelers, swimming more than 10,000 miles (16,000 km) round trip between the lagoons of Baja California where they raise their young and their feeding grounds in the Arctic. But during the 1800s, they were hunted nearly to extinction. Hunting was banned in 1949, and now there are more than 20,000 of them in the eastern Pacific.

Atlantic Puffins

Bright-beaked Atlantic puffins were once a common sight along the coast of Maine in the United States. But by the end of the 19th century, the birds had all but disappeared after they were hunted for their feathers, which were used to stuff pillows and decorate hats. In the 1970s, scientists painstakingly transported eggs from a large colony in Newfoundland, Canada, to Maine, U.S.A. Today, more than 2,000 puffins nest there.

Dugongs

These roly-poly animals were once a prized catch for the fishermen of Madagascar, an island off the southeast coast of Africa—until overhunting caused their population to decrease. In 2007, the region became a marine protected area, and locals report that the gentle creatures are beginning to return to the area once again.

185

Afterword

From high in the sky, astronauts can see what sailors have known for years: The world is *blue!*

More than two-thirds of the surface of our planet is covered by ocean. Clouds circle land and sea; rivers, lakes, and streams lace the land like silver ribbons; snow and ice gleam brightly at the poles. Earth truly is a water planet, a living planet. But from space, from the shore, and even from the surface, what lies below has remained hidden for most of human history.

Explorer Ferdinand Magellan could not have known how large nor how deep the ocean was when he set out to circumnavigate the globe 500 years ago. Many people at that time believed that if ships ventured too far, they would fall off the edge of the Earth. Antarctica was yet to be discovered. Telescopes and microscopes had yet to be invented. Submarines and diving suits were still hundreds of years away.

In 1872, when Britain's H.M.S. *Challenger* set out on the first global expedition to explore the ocean top to bottom, no one had a face mask, flippers, or other equipment to observe sea creatures in their own homes. They could not know about the mighty ranges of undersea mountains, the deep trenches, or the steaming thermal vents. Whales, seals, dolphins, seabirds, cod, tuna, and herring were plentiful, and coral reefs were pristine. Plastics had not yet been invented, nor had airplanes, telephones, or computers, let alone satellite navigation.

By 1972, new technologies had made it possible to go to the moon, to explore the molecular structure of living cells, and yes, even to visit the deepest place in the sea. But it came at a price. The burning of fossil fuels had begun to change the planet's temperature and chemistry, new ways of fishing and new markets for ocean wildlife had caused the decline of many ocean species, and pollution of the world's waters began to awaken concerns. By 2000, nations around the world began to establish marine protected areas, commercial whaling had been banned, and "The Census of Marine Life"—the first global inventory of life in the sea—had gotten underway.

Armed with books like *Beneath the Waves,* today's children have superpowers, knowing what the greatest explorers of the past could not know. Even if you have never seen nor touched the ocean, the ocean touches you with every breath you take: About half of the oxygen in the air comes from life in the sea. Now we know that we are changing the nature of the ocean through what we put into it and what we are taking out. It is also now clear that the greatest era of exploration is just beginning! Even today, most of the ocean has yet to be seen—let alone explored. As never before, this is the time to embrace the ocean with care, and to find a place for ourselves within the mostly blue living systems that make our lives possible.

—Sylvia A. Earle

Sylvia Earle is a marine scientist and National Geographic explorer-in-residence. Earle, who is known as "Her Deepness," has spent thousands of hours under the sea using scuba, living in underwater laboratories, and pioneering the design and use of submersibles and deep-sea robots. She studies marine algae, ocean ecosystems, the behavior of whales, and the role of the living ocean in shaping Earth's climate and chemistry. She was chief scientist of the National Oceanic and Atmospheric Administration and is founder of Deep Ocean Exploration and Research (DOER) and Mission Blue, an organization dedicated to safeguarding the ocean from destructive fishing and pollution with protected areas called "Hope Spots."

SCIENTIFIC NAMES OF OCEAN LIFE

INDEX

INDEX

PHOTO CREDITS

AL=Alamy Stock Photo; AS=Adobe Stock; GI=Getty Images; NGIC=National Geographic Image Collection; SS=Shutterstock

Cover: (sea turtle), Brian J. Skerry/NGIC; (watercolor), Zodiact/SS; back cover, Thomas P. Peschak/NGIC; paper texture (throughout), YamabikaY/SS; Polaroid frames (throughout), darkbird/AS; brushstroke frame (throughout), Lustrator/SS; **Front matter:** 1, Toshiko Tamura/EyeEm/GI; 2-3, lunamarina/AS; 4-5, Pommeyrol Vincent/SS; 6, Luis Lamar/NGIC; 8 (UP LE), Oleksandrum/AS; 8 (UP RT), Reinhard Dirscherl/GI; 8 (LO LE), Ivanova Tetyana/SS; 8 (LO CTR), M.Photos/SS; 8 (LO RT), tunart/GI; 8 (background), Sonya92/SS; 9 (UP), leonardogonzalez/AS; 9 (LO LE), Paul Nicklen/NGIC; 9 (LO RT), David Doubilet/NGIC; 9 (background), AnjeseAnna/SS; 10-11, Rachel McNaughton; **On the Beach:** watercolor background (throughout), Sonya92/SS; watercolor circle (throughout), Zodiact/SS; 12-13, tilialucida/AS; 14 (LE), Oleksandrum/AS; 14 (RT), Pinopic/GI; 15, PhotoStock-Israel/GI; 16 (LE), Morales/GI; 16 (RT), hinnamsaisuy/SS; 17 (UP), MShieldsPhotos/AL; 17 (LO LE), Jurgen Freund/Nature Picture Library; 17 (LO RT), David Persson/SS; 18-19, Kelly Taylor/AL; 20, Jason Edwards/NGIC; 22 (LE), Alex Hyde/Minden Pictures; 22 (RT), mario pesce/SS; 23 (UP LE), George Ostertag/AL; 23 (UP RT), Clement Philippe/AL; 23 (LO), Sara Montour Lewis/Cavan Social/AS; 24 (LE), BirdImages/GI; 24 (RT), Dmitry Deshevykh/GI; 25 (UP LE), Peter Essick/NGIC; 25 (UP RT), Red ivory/SS; 25 (LO), Elizabeth Netterstrom/SS; 26 (UP LE), vectorkat/SS; 26 (UP CTR), darsi/AS; 26 (UP RT), Anja Kaiser/AS; 26 (RT), nimon_t/AS; 26-27 (background), fajno/AS; 27 (UP LE), Nadzeya_Kizilava/GI; 27 (UP RT), vvvita/AS; 27 (LO), Shur_ca/GI; **Between Two Worlds:** watercolor background (throughout), Sonya92/SS; watercolor circle (throughout), ilolab/SS; 28-29, Michael Szoenyi/imageBROKER/AS; 30, Discover Marco/SS; 32, Brian J. Skerry/NGIC; 33, Lisa Graham/All Canada Photos; 34 (LE), BMJ/SS; 34 (RT), Rudmer Zwerver/SS; 35 (UP LE), Christian Musat/AS; 35 (UP RT), Robin Chittenden/Minden Pictures; 35 (LO), Ralph Lee Hopkins/NGIC; 36, flownaksala/AS; 37, Joost van Uffelen/SS; 38-39, Alexander Machulskiy/SS; 40 (LE), G. Lacz/Arco/AL; 40 (RT), Tim Laman/NGIC; 41 (UP LE), Anthony Pierce/AL; 41 (UP RT), J'nel/SS; 41 (LO), Paulo Oliveira/AL; 42 (UP), Eskymaks/AS; 42 (LO), Franco Tempesta; 42 (map background), javarman/AS; 42-43 (scroll background), Roman Sigaev/AS; 43, nimon_t/AS; **Wading In:** watercolor background (throughout), Elena_Design/SS; watercolor circle (throughout), Katsiaryna Chumakova/SS; 44-45, Ferenc/AS; 46, johnandersonphoto/GI; 47, SeaTops/imageBROKER/SS; 48 (LE), naturediver/AS; 48 (RT), roc8jas/GI; 49 (UP), Michael Zeigler/GI; 49 (LO LE), Reinhard Dirscherl/AL; 49 (LO RT), Ethan Daniels/SS; 50, MWolf Images/AS; 51, Carol Visser/EyeEm/GI; 52 (LE), Cingular/SS; 52 (RT), Wes C. Skiles/NGIC; 53 (UP), Danté Fenolio/Science Source; 53 (LO LE), Mathieu Meur/Stocktrek Images/GI; 53 (LO RT), f11photo/SS; 54 (UP LE), vectorkat/SS; 54 (UP CTR), darsi/AS; 54 (UP RT), Anja Kaiser/AS; 54 (RT), nimon_t/AS; 54-55 (background), fajno/AS; 55 (UP LE), Mauricio Handler/NGIC; 55 (UP RT), cinoby/GI; 55 (LO),

Historical Images Archive/AL; **Reef Life:** watercolor background (throughout), Sonya92/SS; watercolor circle (throughout), ilolab/SS; 56-57, ifish/GI; 58, Little Dinosaur/GI; 59, acro_phuket/SS; 60, Design Pics Inc/NGIC; 61, Wendy A. Capili/GI; 62-63, Stocktrek Images/NGIC; 64 (UP LE), vectorkat/SS; 64 (UP CTR), darsi/AS; 64 (UP RT), Anja Kaiser/AS; 64 (RT & LO LE), nimon_t/AS; 64-65 (background), fajno/AS; 65 (UP LE), NASA/GSFC/LaRC/JPL, MISR Team; 65 (UP RT), Historical Picture Archive/Corbis/Corbis via GI; 65 (LO LE), Werner Forman/Universal Images Group/GI; 65 (LO RT), DeAgostini/N. Cirani/GI; 66 (LE), richcarey/GI; 66 (RT), frantisekhojdysz/SS; 67 (UP), Yann-HUBERT/GI; 67 (LO LE), Norbert Probst/AL; 67 (LO RT), Global_Pics/GI; 68, Norbert Probst/AL; 69, Jay Dickman/NGIC; 70, Masa Ushioda/AL; 73, Westend61/GI; **Ocean Forests:** watercolor background (throughout), ami mataraj/SS; watercolor circle (throughout), KarolinaCloud/SS; 74-75, Tim Laman/NGIC; 76 (LE), RooM The Agency/AS; 76 (RT), Brian J. Skerry/NGIC; 77, damedias/AS; 78-79, Michael Zeigler/GI; 80, Alastair Pollock Photography/GI; 81, Mathieu Foulquie/Biosphoto/AL; 82, Brook/AS; 84, Paul Nicklen/NGIC; 85, David Courtenay/GI; 86 (LE), cherylvb/AS; 86 (RT), Design Pics Inc/NGIC; 87 (UP), Barbara Ash/AL; 87 (LO LE), Ken Lucas/GI; 87 (LO RT), Jon Gross Photography/AL; 88, joebelanger/GI; 90 (UP), Eskymaks/AS; 90 (LO), TriggerPhoto/GI; 90 (map background), javarman/AS; 90-91 (scroll background), Roman Sigaev/AS; 91, nimon_t/AS; **The Open Ocean:** watercolor background (throughout), AnjeseAnna/SS; watercolor circle (throughout), Elena_Design/SS; 92-93, Dave Fleetham/GI; 94-95, eco2drew/GI; 96-97, Paul Nicklen/NGIC; 97, Jeffrey Rotman/AL; 98 (LE), inusuke/GI; 98 (RT), Richard Herrmann/Visuals Unlimited, Inc./GI; 99 (UP), Thomas P. Peschak/NGIC; 99 (LO LE), Cristina Mittermeier/NGIC; 99 (LO RT), Irina K./AS; 100-101, leonardogonzalez/AS; 102, Richard Carey/AS; 104, Jeff Wildermuth/NGIC; 105, Brian J. Skerry/NGIC; 106 (LE), Dante Fenolio/GI; 106 (RT), Nielsdk/imageBROKER/SS; 107 (UP), martin_hristov/SS; 107 (LO LE), Paulo Oliveira/AL; 107 (LO RT), paulbcowell/GI; 108 (UP LE), Eskymaks/AS; 108 (UP RT), Science History Images/AL; 108 (LO), The History Collection/AL; 108 (map background), javarman/AS; 108-109 (scroll background), Roman Sigaev/AS; 109, nimon_t/AS; **On the Move:** watercolor background (throughout), ami mataraj/SS; watercolor circle (throughout), Sonya92/SS; 110-111, Janos/AS; 112-113, Michel Roggo/Nature Picture Library; 114 (LE), Alexander Safonov/GI; 114 (RT), Mark Conlin/AL; 115 (UP), wildestanimal/SS; 115 (LO LE), Paul/AS; 115 (LO RT), Alessandro De Maddalena/SS; 116, Brian J. Skerry/NGIC; 118 (LE), Karl Van Ginderdeuren/Minden Pictures; 118 (RT), Mauricio Handler/NGIC; 119 (UP), wildestanimal/GI; 119 (LO LE), Alex Mustard/Nature Picture Library; 119 (LO RT), a_m_radul/AS; 120-121, Larry Beard; 122 (LE), Marc Guyt/AL; 122 (RT), CORNU Laurent/SS; 123 (UP), Jukka Jantunen/SS; 123 (LO LE), Hakoar/Dreamstime; 123 (LO RT), Daniela Duncan/GI; 124 (UP), Eskymaks/AS; 124 (LO), digitalbalance/SS; 124 (map background), javarman/AS; 124-125 (scroll background), Roman Sigaev/AS; 125, nimon_t/AS; **Life on the Icy Edge:** watercolor background (throughout), Margo-sirin/SS; watercolor circle (throughout), Pimelar/SS; 126-127, Paul Nicklen/NGIC; 128 (LE), KeithSzafranski/GI; 128 (RT), Joseph Van Os/GI; 129, Paul Nicklen/NGIC; 130 (LE), Laurent Ballesta/NGIC; 130 (RT), Brian J. Skerry/NGIC; 131 (UP), Ralph Lee Hopkins/NGIC; 131 (LO LE), Paul Souders/GI; 131 (LO RT),

Paul Nicklen/NGIC; 132-133, Ralph Lee Hopkins/NGIC; 133, Alexey Seafarer/AS; 134-135, Paul Nicklen/NGIC; 136 (LE), Flip Nicklin/Minden Pictures; 136 (RT), Jordi Chias/Minden Pictures; 137 (UP), Rob Robbins/USAP/National Science Foundation; 137 (LO LE), Flip Nicklin/Minden Pictures; 137 (LO RT), David Tipling/AL; 138 (UP), Eskymaks/AS; 138 (LO), Cristina Mittermeier/NGIC; 138 (map background), javarman/AS; 138-139 (scroll background), Roman Sigaev/AS; 139, nimon_t/AS; **Deep Down:** watercolor background (throughout), tsyhun/SS; watercolor circle (throughout), Katsiaryna Chumakova/SS; 140-141, Paul Nicklen/NGIC; 142, Laurent Ballesta/NGIC; 143, Uli Kunz/NGIC; 144-145, David_Slater/GI; 146 (LE), Paulo Oliveira/AL; 146 (RT), Jennifer Berglund; 147 (UP), Norbert Wu/Minden Pictures; 147 (LO LE), David Liittschwager/NGIC; 147 (LO RT), David Shale/Nature Picture Library; 148 (LE), E. Widder/HBOI/GI; 148 (RT), Noriaki Yamamoto/Minden Pictures; 149 (UP), Steve Downer/Science Source; 149 (LO LE), The Natural History Museum/AL; 149 (LO RT), Norbert Wu/Minden Pictures; 150, David Shale/Minden Pictures; 151, diveivanov/AS; 152, superjoseph/AS; 154 (LE), Franco Banfi/GI; 154 (RT), David Shen/Blue Planet Archive; 155 (UP LE), Brandon Cole Marine Photography/AL; 155 (UP RT), Bill Curtsinger/NGIC; 155 (LO), Kelvin Aitken/Image Quest Marine; 156 (UP), Eskymaks/AS; 156 (LO), Thomas J. Abercrombie/NGIC; 156 (map background), javarman/AS; 156-157 (scroll background), Roman Sigaev/AS; 157, nimon_t/AS; **Extreme Ocean:** watercolor background (throughout), Suto Norbert Zsolt/SS; watercolor circle (throughout), Zodiact/SS; 158-159, Brian J. Skerry/NGIC; 160 (UP LE), vectorkat/SS; 160 (UP CTR), darsi/AS; 160 (UP RT), Anja Kaiser/AS; 160 (RT), nimon_t/AS; 160-161 (background), fajno/AS; 161 (UP LE), Historia/REX/SS; 161 (UP RT), FLPA/SS; 161 (LO), duncan1890/GI; 162-163, DirkR/AS; 163 (UP), Tomas Kotouc/AS; 163 (LO LE), Emory Kristof/NGIC; 163 (LO RT), courtesy of NOAA; 164, Emory Kristof/NGIC; 165 (UP), courtesy of NOAA Okeanos Explorer Program, Galapagos Rift Expedition 2011; 165 (LO LE), Reinhard Dirscherl/imageBROKER/SS; 165 (LO RT), David Shale/Nature Picture Library; 166, David Doubilet/NGIC; 167 (UP), Brian J. Skerry/NGIC; 167 (LO), Jennifer Idol/Stocktrek Images/GI; 168 (UP), Eskymaks/AS; 168 (LO), Granger.com - All rights reserved; 168 (map background), javarman/AS; 168-169 (scroll background), Roman Sigaev/AS; 169, nimon_t/AS; **People and Oceans:** watercolor background (throughout), Elina Li/SS; watercolor circle (throughout), Katsiaryna Chumakova/SS; 170-171, anekoho/SS; 172 (UP LE), Album/British Library/AL; 172 (UP RT), John Cairns/AL; 172 (LO), Perry Thorsvik/NGIC; 173 (UP LE), John Tee-Van/NGIC; 173 (UP RT), Luis Marden/NGIC; 173 (LO), Charles Nicklin/NGIC; 175, Ozbalci/GI; 176-177, Joel Sartore/NGIC; 179, Avi Kalpfer/NGIC; 180 (LO LE), Ivanova Tetyana/SS; 180 (LO RT), M.Photos/SS; 180-181 (background), Alexander Nikitin/SS; 181 (tape), Picsfive/SS; 181 (UP LE), Kike Ballesteros/SS; 181 (UP RT), Dave McAloney/NGIC; 181 (LO), Andy Mann/NGIC; 182-183, panaramka/AS; 183, Elyse Butler; 184 (LE), scubanine/SS; 184 (RT), Joe Belanger/SS; 185 (UP), Mark Conlin/GI; 185 (LO LE), lemga/GI; 185 (LO RT), Guy Bryant/AS; 186, David Doubilet/NGIC; **Back matter:** watercolor background (throughout), Elina Li/SS; 189, Steven Hunt/GI; 192, Alex Mustard/Nature Picture Library; **Endsheets:** Zodiact/SS

FOR BRYAR, WITH ALL MY LOVE —S.W.D.

Since 1888, the National Geographic Society has funded more than 12,000 research, exploration, and preservation projects around the world. The Society receives funds from National Geographic Partners, LLC, funded in part by your purchase. A portion of the proceeds from this book supports this vital work. To learn more, visit natgeo.com/info.

For more information, visit nationalgeographic.com, call 1-877-873-6846, or write to the following address:

National Geographic Partners
1145 17th Street N.W.
Washington, D.C. 20036-4688 U.S.A.

Visit us online at nationalgeographic.com/books

For librarians and teachers: nationalgeographic.com/books/librarians-and-educators/

More for kids from National Geographic: natgeokids.com

National Geographic Kids magazine inspires children to explore their world with fun yet educational articles on animals, science, nature, and more. Using fresh storytelling and amazing photography, *Nat Geo Kids* shows kids ages 6 to 14 the fascinating truth about the world—and why they should care. **kids.nationalgeographic.com/subscribe**

For rights or permissions inquiries, please contact National Geographic Books Subsidiary Rights: bookrights@natgeo.com

Designed by Brett Challos

The publisher would like to acknowledge the following people for making this book possible: Priyanka Lamichhane, senior editor; Shelby Lees, senior editor; Libby Romero, senior editor; Jen Agresta, project editor; Stephanie Warren Drimmer, author; Brett Challos, art director; Lori Epstein, photo director; Hilary Andrews, associate photo editor; Joan Gossett, editorial production manager; Alix Inchausti, production editor; Anne LeongSon and Gus Tello, design production assistants; Michelle Harris, fact-checker.

The publisher would also like to thank Rick Keil and Khadijah Homolka, University of Washington School of Oceanography, for their expert review of the manuscript.

Hardcover ISBN: 978-1-4263-3916-5
Reinforced library binding ISBN: 978-1-4263-3917-2

Printed in Hong Kong
20/PPHK/1